"Suffering set Sara Walker free ~~~~~~~~~~~~~
completely—to savor the moments that most of us ~~~~~~~
The Light Shines Through, Sara has painted a masterpiece that painfully and wonderfully explores God's transforming and redeeming grace, not despite, but through our suffering. But this is not her magnum opus. No, her greatest work was not her labor at all, but rather the work of God in answering her prayers. Sara's touching story resonates deeply with my own experience and observation of suffering."

—**Dr. Kent Brantly,** Ebola survivor and coauthor of *Called for Life*

"I wish everyone could have known Sara, both the young Sara I met when I was just eight years old and the adult Sara who battled cancer with such absolute grace. Now, because of this book, people can do just that. This book will bring *hope* to so many lives because, in Sara's own elegant voice, it reflects her most timeless quality: her pureness of heart."

—**Kyle Jackson,** Executive Teaching Pastor, Next Level Church, Ft. Myers, FL

"We *are* our stories. And Sara's story is fully, authentically, terribly, sadly, and beautifully human. It is also fully and triumphantly Christian. Although no two stories are exactly alike, sharing them emboldens and nurtures us along the journey. Read through your tears and discover the story of a godly woman who found God faithful. Be encouraged for whatever lies ahead. The same God who sustained Sara is there for all who seek him."

—**Rubel Shelly,** Professor of Philosophy and Bible, Lipscomb University

"This is one of the most powerful stories I have ever read or observed. As a father who has lost a young son, this book helped me in ways that nothing else has. It allowed the truths of God's Word, his promises, his mercy, to push through the tremendous pain of grief and loss. It gave me hope and insight into life, loss, and death. Sara's story will inspire you to live every moment for the Lord and others no matter what."

—**Mitch Temple,** Executive Director for The Fatherhood CoMission, consultant and marketing specialist for over 30 Christian movies, including *Courageous* and *War Room*

"Grieving the loss of her daughter and battling cancer, Sara courageously and gracefully shared the honest cries of her heart. Her words inspired thousands through her Caring Bridge blog posts. *The Light Shines Through* continues that legacy of faith. As you read, prepare to laugh, cry, and be reminded that no matter what you are going through, he is there and his light shines through."

—Tom Norvell, counselor, speaker, life coach, author of *A Norvell Note*

"Sara saw beyond the obvious, day-to-day things, and she learned to be still and focus on God's eternal truths. This story demonstrates the abundant way that her life impacted others. It is an uplifting testimony of a transparent individual who savored the day, put others first, demonstrated God's love and guidance, and yet dealt with the emotions and challenges that are part of life. Take the time to read Sara's story. It will be a blessing."

—John S. Halle, PT, PhD, ECS, Professor, School of Physical Therapy, Belmont University

"This is not an abstract discussion of faith. It is human and real. And while you'll surely feel the sadness and loss of Sara's story, you'll be moved by her love and hope. You'll be blown away by her strength."

—Gin Phillips, author of *The Well and the Mine* and *Fierce Kingdom*

"A diagnosis of cancer is life-altering. How that patient emerges from that initial shock and finds the strength to move forward amazes me every day. Sara Walker was a patient who fought with passion, grace, and a fierce love of life that made an impact on everyone around her. In this beautiful testament, Sara shows us her emotional and spiritual journey. In life her writings inspired and comforted many, and through this book she will continue to help others."

—Johanna Bendell, MD, Sarah Cannon Research Institute

As a young girl, Sara dreamed of being a writer—someone whose words would encourage many hearts while shining the spotlight on her loving Heavenly Father. Sara's dream came true in an unexpected way. Her cancer led to a blog that was visited nearly a million times in just eighteen months! As a result, countless hearts have been encouraged. *The Light Shines Through* beautifully shares Sara's gift of writing and provides a glimpse into her inspiring life."

—Walt Leaver, Minister, Brentwood Hills Church of Christ

The Light Shines Through

A Story
of Hope
in the Midst
of Suffering

Sara Walker

with J. Heyward Rogers

L E A F W O O D
P U B L I S H E R S
an imprint of Abilene Christian University Press

THE LIGHT SHINES THROUGH

A Story of Hope in the Midst of Suffering

L E A F W O O D
P U B L I S H E R S
an imprint of Abilene Christian University Press

Copyright © 2018 by Sara Walker

ISBN 978-1-68426-040-9 | LCCN 2017044229

Printed in the United States of America

LIBRARY OF CONGRESS CATALOGING-IN-PUBLICATION DATA
Names: Walker, Sara, 1978-2012, author.
Title: The light shines through : a story of hope in the midst of suffering /
    by Sara Walker, with J. Heyward Rogers.
Description: Abilene : Leafwood Publishers, 2018.
Identifiers: LCCN 2017044229 | ISBN 9781684260409 (pbk.)
Subjects: LCSH: Consolation. | Walker, Sara, 1978-2012. |
    Cancer—Patients—Religious life.
Classification: LCC BV4910.33 .W35 2018 | DDC 276.8/55092 [B]—dc23

Cover design by ThinkPen Designs | Interior text design by Sandy Armstrong, Strong Design

Leafwood Publishers is an imprint of Abilene Christian University Press
ACU Box 29138, Abilene, Texas 79699

1-877-816-4455 | www.leafwoodpublishers.com

18 19 20 21 22 23 / 7 6 5 4 3 2 1

Contents

Preface

It had only been a week since Sara Walker had been diagnosed with terminal cancer, only seven weeks since she had lost her own baby Anna at thirty-eight weeks' gestation. Her friend Jennifer marveled, therefore, at Sara's reaction the first time she saw Jennifer's newborn daughter. "Look at those beautiful eyes," Sara said. "God gave you those eyes to see. And look at those ears. God gave you those ears to hear."

That was Sara Walker in a nutshell. She saw things differently, and she caused other people to see things differently, too. Everybody else saw a cute little baby. They looked to see whether she had her mother's eyes, her father's nose. But Sara looked deeper and saw a human being, formed in the image of God, embarking on a lifetime in which the beauties of God would be poured out before her—but a life in which she would have to open her eyes if she wanted to see those marvels. Everybody who saw Jennifer's baby noticed her beautiful eyes. Sara saw something else: those winsome eyes were also portals through which God's beauty would enter and beautify her further still. Sara's words over that baby were both a blessing and a charge: *Look. Listen. Take in this world where God has placed you, and see that the Lord is good.*

That wasn't just Sara Walker's message to one baby. It was her message to everyone who met her and to the hundreds of thousands of visitors who read her blog in the two years after her diagnosis. Her unique vision—clarified and sharpened by great suffering—and her ability to give voice to her vision changed the way countless people look at the world where God has placed them. "Savor the day," Sara told them, over and over again. As her days on earth grew fewer and fewer, she learned to savor them more intensely, knowing that the joys of this world are but a shadow of the New Heaven and New Earth, knowing also that the sufferings of this world (and Sara knew those intensely as well) will one day seem light as a feather next to the eternal weight of glory that awaits us.

Through her Caring Bridge blog and her *Savoring the Day* blog, Sara lived the hardest months of her life in full view of others. Her courage made them more courageous; the strength of her faith strengthened their faith. But the secret ingredient of Sara's writing was her honesty. When she struggled with discouragement, when she felt let down by God and she doubted his goodness, she wrote about it with full transparency. Even in her disappointment and doubt, she knew that disappointment and doubt would not have the last word. She wrote with the heart of a psalmist—"My God, my God, why have you forsaken me?" (Ps. 22:1)—and with the win-win attitude of Paul—"For to me, to live is Christ, and to die is gain. . . . Yet what shall I choose? I do not know! I am torn between the two" (Phil. 1:21-22).

In May of 2010, Sara Walker started praying a dangerous prayer. Her life at the time seemed rather average; she would even have described her life as unremarkable. She was a thirty-two-year-old wife and mother of two boys. A third baby was on the way, a little girl named Anna, who was due in December of that year. When she was younger, Sara had dreamed of being a writer, but that dream had been on hold for a long time. Her ministry was at church and at the physical therapy clinic where she was a therapist. Her family and friends saw tremendous gifts and extraordinary faith in her. They admired the way she ministered tirelessly within her spheres of influence. But Sara had the nagging feeling that God meant for her to have a broader ministry. Something was holding her back from the bold, sold-out life of the Christians she admired most. Was it fear? Perfectionism? Pride? Low self-esteem? She started praying a prayer she learned from a sermon her minister preached that spring: "God, let me make a difference for you that is utterly disproportionate to who I am." It's a simple prayer, but it's oh so powerful.

"God, let me make a difference for you that is utterly disproportionate to who I am." God began to answer that prayer later that year, but not in a way Sara could have predicted.

On December 6, 2010, two weeks before her due date, Sara's baby died in the womb. It was the seventh wedding anniversary of Sara and her husband Brian. "My ways are not your ways," says the Lord, "nor are my thoughts your thoughts" (Isa. 55:8). Sometimes God's mercies are severe. Losing Anna was a heavy blow for Sara and Brian, as well as the rest of the family. But heavier blows soon would come.

Exactly six weeks after Anna's stillbirth, Sara was in the hospital again. She went to the emergency room after experiencing chest pains. When the doctors looked at her chest x-rays, they noticed something odd. Part of Sara's liver was in the frame, and it didn't look good. Upon further investigation, they realized that Sara's liver was full of metastasized cancer. That is to say, not only was there a lot of cancer in her liver, but that cancer hadn't started in her liver; it had spread from elsewhere in her body.

On January 20, her thirty-third birthday, Sara got her official diagnosis: Stage IV colon cancer. There are only four stages. This diagnosis was as serious as a cancer diagnosis gets.

Sara was feeling like Job in the Bible. From a human perspective, her afflictions were as inexplicable as Job's. Anna had been perfectly healthy until the day she died, still inside Sara's body. Sara herself had seemed perfectly healthy, with no pain whatsoever, until the day she discovered that her body had already been ravaged by cancer. Anna's death and Sara's illness both seemed to come out of the blue, like the troubles God allowed Satan to visit on Job in that old, old story.

On her second visit to the oncologist—the visit when she went to get the results of her liver biopsy—Sara signed in and sat down with her father. The next patient called was a man named Mr. Job, pronounced just like the Job in the Bible. In that time of bewilderment and sorrow, Sara and her father took it as a little wink from God, and they hoped and prayed it was a sign that her story would end like Job's: "And the Lord blessed the latter days of Job more than his beginning. . . . And Job died, an old man full of days" (Job 42:12, 17 ESV).

Sara had prayed that her life would make a disproportionate impact for the Kingdom of God. She got the death of a child and a terminal cancer diagnosis. If these were answers to her prayer, they were decidedly not the answers she was looking for. Yet it soon became clear that these afflictions were very much the beginning of God's answer because Sara Walker soon began to make an impact that was far out of proportion to who she had ever thought she was.

A week after receiving her diagnosis, Sara started a blog at CaringBridge.com, a site created to allow people battling extensive illnesses to keep family and friends updated on their "health journey." But Sara had a somewhat different vision for her little corner of Caring Bridge. Yes, she gave concerned readers regular updates on her "health journey," but Sara's Caring Bridge site was really about her spiritual journey, as is obvious from her very first entry:

> In awe. Overwhelmed. Thankful. Fearful. So many, many emotions competing within me these days. Thank you all for reminding me of God's power and his goodness. I need to be reminded of that truth frequently right now. We are still facing many decisions at this point. I know I need to do my part, but I believe God is guiding our steps and that if he wants to heal, he can do so through any means.

Understand that while I try to stay positive and allow the peace of Christ to rule in my heart, I do have rough times. Last night I got on my knees, face to the floor, and sobbed. I begged with all my might for God to heal me so that I can live to help my husband raise our boys. So that I can live to share the story of his mercy for many years to come. My God is big enough to handle my fears, and he asks me to lay my burdens at his feet. What I'm still learning is how to leave them there.

This morning, I am refreshed. Through that prayer, through the sunshine outside today, through the Spirit inside me, and through your encouraging messages, he has filled me with *the peace* yet again.

Please pray for our decisions.

From day one, Sara put her readers on notice. Her battle was not "against flesh and blood, but against the rulers, against the authorities, against the cosmic powers over this present darkness, against the spiritual forces of evil in the heavenly places" (Eph. 6:12 ESV).

The more Sara wrote, the more honest and transparent she became, and people started to notice. They started sharing her posts with others; by the spring of 2012, Sara's sites had received four hundred sixty thousand visits. A worldwide community took shape, people sharing Sara's journey and learning to see things differently, the way Sara was learning to see things. Thanks to Sara, thousands of people learned to savor the days they had. Like the newborn daughter of Sara's friend, they heard that their eyes were for seeing and their ears were for hearing the things that God had put in their lives to point them back to himself.

Sara came to view her thirty-third birthday as the birthday of the New Sara. Her terminal diagnosis, far from paralyzing her with terror, set her free from the fear of man, the fear of failure, the fear of being less than perfect or appearing less than perfectly put together. It showed her that all those things she had always said she believed about the love of Jesus turned out to be truer than she had ever known. It showed her that even her doubts about God's goodness were no match for his overpowering love. Her terminal diagnosis opened her up to speak the truth in love in ways that she never had before.

This book tells the story of Sara's journey in those difficult but beautiful last two years of her earthly life. As much as possible, it will tell her story in her own words.

"Now the LORD blessed the latter days of Job more than His beginning. . . . And Job died, an old man, and full of days" (Job 42:12, 17). When Sara Walker died, she wasn't old. She wasn't what the Bible calls "full of days." But from her cancer diagnosis to the end, her days were full of life. She made sure of that. And her latter days, like those of Job, were more blessed than her beginning. For God had answered her prayers. He allowed her to make an impact that was disproportionate to who she was.

Chapter One

Anna

Editor's Note: Sara began writing a book telling her own story. This chapter is the first chapter from that book. Her declining health made it impossible for her to continue; instead, she poured all her writing energies into her blog posts. Subsequent chapters have been assembled from Sara's blog posts and interviews with her family and friends and have been edited for publication. But this one is all Sara.

They describe it as a lightness, like flying. They say that when your worst fears materialize right in front of your eyes, you go into shock. Many say it's like floating outside of your body, watching as if from a distance the nightmare that is playing out in reality.

That's not what I experienced. And I've experienced it twice now. At two distinct moments in my life, in the span of only one month, my worst fears were realized.

There was no lightness, no floating. Only an extreme heaviness, a sense of being immovable. I was rooted to the spot with thick, gnarled roots that had twisted over me, entangled me, and then sunk themselves deep, deep into the earth.

They say you feel disconnected. Outside of yourself. But never before have I ever felt so present, so aware, so alive, so mortal. The unbinding, the freedom, the lightness, the flying—oh, that would come. That would come later, with the joyful surrender.

But they are right about one thing. There is another presence, a separate presence. There are two distinct beings in that space and time.

He was there. The Son of God was there. Right beside me, in front of me, behind me, inside of me. All places at once. Permeating my being. Surrounding me. Shielding me.

He whispered, "You will feel this, my child. I will not keep you from experiencing this. But it will not consume you. I will take the worst blows. I will absorb the worst of this pain for you. You will feel, but only a fraction. We will endure this attack together, and then you will watch and wonder. You will watch in awe as I fight back, as I defend you. This is not your battle. The battle is mine. Watch in wonder, my precious child."

It had been a dark weekend. Anna had stilled inside me.

In December of 2010, I was nearing the end of my third pregnancy. Life was happy. I had two sons, ages five and three, and they were anxious to welcome home a new baby sister. I was little more than two weeks away from the due date, and all had gone perfectly smoothly up to this point. It had been a completely uneventful pregnancy, with all tests, all screens, all ultrasounds revealing a perfectly healthy baby girl growing in all the right ways inside me. I saw the doctor for a routine check on Tuesday. All was well.

By Friday, everything had changed.

It began that Friday morning, just seventeen days before her due date. That Friday morning, instead of awakening to Anna's gentle nudges inside my belly, I woke up to stillness. I lay in bed for hours, anxiously awaiting movement, some sign of life. I poked and prodded my belly, willing her to wake up and give me a good hard kick back. Nothing came; only empty stillness. Somehow I knew.

I tried to choke back the terrifying thought that she was gone, reminding myself that the doctor had assured me that the odds of any problems at all this late in pregnancy were in the million-to-one range. Maybe she had just grown too big to move around; maybe she had just dropped low enough in the birth canal that she was now wedged in place, unable to so much as wiggle. But somehow, *somehow*, I knew.

I finally decided to get up and eat breakfast, thinking that if I stirred, she would awaken. Sometime in the late morning, it happened. I finally felt a flicker from deep within—three faint, small hiccup-like flutters at the top of my belly. This was not where I typically felt movement, but my heart seized at the chance, at the hope. A tiny hope flickered in my heart—small, as faint as the movement had been, but there. I clung to hope as if on a cliff, hanging on by slipping fingertips, trying not to gaze down at the vast abyss of sorrow beneath me.

Those were the last movements I would feel.

I didn't call the doctor. Perhaps I was afraid of what I would find out. I convinced myself I was overreacting. I should have faith. I should trust. After all, at the last appointment, a mere three days ago, she'd been fine. Her heart was strong. I had no history of miscarriage whatsoever and had already had two completely healthy pregnancies before. There was absolutely no precedent for anything other than a normal healthy Anna to be arriving in only a few days.

Saturday morning, the stillness remained. I worried, I prayed—but had I not prayed enough? *Oh, my baby girl, perhaps I didn't pray over you enough . . .*

I felt a deep, penetrating sadness most of Saturday. I didn't accomplish much that day, ever waiting to feel her move.

Nothing. Stillness.

Saturday night I played with my sons at bedtime. We shared a Bible story. We spoke memory verses. We prayed for Anna to be safe. Shortly after tucking them in bed, the labor began. My body began to shake. Chills ran up and down my body and would not stop. I could not get warm—not in the scalding hot shower, not under many blankets, not with my husband Brian holding me, trying to give his body heat to me, his trembling, weeping wife. As I look back now, I think the last of Anna's life force must have finally left my body, leaving me cold. Empty and cold. So cold.

The thermometer revealed I had a fever, but it was not all that high. I took what I could in the way of medicine and then shivered throughout the night, long after the fever had broken. I didn't know it then, of course, but Anna was gone from me, and her warmth had gone with her. My body physically longed to have her back.

Sunday was more of the same. I didn't go to church because of my fever. Maybe it was an excuse. I methodically, numbly "nested" all day instead. I did laundry. I packed my hospital bag. I packed the boys' bags for their trip to Nana's. Brian brought in the bassinet to set up in our bedroom. But it was all so mechanical. We felt no excitement, no joy as we prepared for her arrival. My attitude had filtered to Brian's, I think. Sunday night the chills began again.

Monday morning, I got the boys ready for preschool and got myself ready for work. I robotically drove to work, parked my car, walked inside. I would later have no remembrance of where I'd parked; I was that preoccupied.

I knew I was going to call my OB first thing. His office is in the same building where I work, and I passed his office door on the way to my office. As I passed, I was relieved to see that people were already in the waiting room; I could call their office immediately and speak to someone besides the answering service.

I walked upstairs to my office. Our administrative staff person, my dear friend Angie, said, "You made it." My co-workers were expecting me to go into labor at any point, because I was huge.

"Yep, I made it," I said flatly, without emotion. "I'm here, anyway." I went to my desk in the back, stored my belongings, and turned on my computer. I took a deep breath. It was time to do what I'd been avoiding doing all weekend. It was time to face this. I dialed the doctor's office.

"Yes, this is Sara Walker. Dr. Burch is my doctor. I'm thirty-eight weeks pregnant. I didn't feel the baby move this past weekend. I know that's something you want us to let you know about."

Please, please, make me feel ridiculous for calling. Please, please be rude. Please say, "Of course you haven't felt the

17

baby move, it has gotten big and dropped down into the birth canal." Please say, "That's not an emergency. We'll see you on your next scheduled visit."

"Oh, okay, wait a second, Sara. Let me ask the nurse; she's standing right here."

A terrible pause.

"Yes, she says come on in as soon as you can. Just get here."

No, no, no, no. This is not happening. This is a bad sign. A bad sign.

"Oh, okay. Um, well, I work just upstairs, so I could come right on down there now." Another pause while the receptionist checked with the nurse.

"Rhonda says come on down. Dr. Burch won't be here until 9:15, but Rhonda can still get started with vitals so he's ready to see you as soon as he gets here."

This was not how the conversation was supposed to go. This was not good; they had never addressed my questions so quickly over the phone. They'd never had me come in so immediately. As if in a fog, I walked to the front of our clinic. I explained to our assistant staffer that I had to go down to my doctor's office so they could check the baby, and I needed her to cover my first patients for me.

I walked out with only my purse, determined I suppose, that I would be returning soon to get back to my workday, because the baby would be fine. She was fine, I told myself.

The nightmare had begun.

I signed in at Dr. Burch's office and sat down in the waiting room. I closed my eyes and I prayed. *Maybe if I just pray enough, if I just pray the right words, all this will stop; I will wake up from this nightmare.* My eyes stayed closed. I didn't care what anyone else in that waiting room thought. The world had closed in on me. I saw no one, noticed nothing. I was isolated and suffocating. I begged God. I pleaded. I begged him to spare my baby girl, my only baby girl.

The nurse, Rhonda, called me back. She checked all the normal things, then took me to a room and told me to undress. A few seconds later she came back and said, "Actually, Dr. Burch wants to go ahead and start with an ultrasound."

Not good! my brain screamed. *Why are we starting with an ultrasound?* My mere description of the weekend was enough to cause serious concern. I undressed, alone in the cold pink ultrasound room, and lay down on the cold table. These are my memories of that time—darkness and cold. Always cold. I waited and prayed.

Dr. Burch and Rhonda came into the room. As Dr. Burch started the ultrasound, he asked me to repeat what had happened over the weekend. I looked at the screen as Anna's body appeared. I saw her spine, arched perfectly. I searched along the hollow blackness underneath it for the pounding, the expanding and shrinking shadow of the heartbeat. Again there was only stillness, darkness, emptiness. I watched for fifteen seconds at the most, maybe not more than five. Dr. Burch asked me to reposition. Another bad sign. He had not seen what he'd hoped to see. There was a long pause as he searched, frequently moving the ultrasound head to a different spot, searching intensely, methodically.

Too long. Too long. It shouldn't be taking this long. It wouldn't take this long if everything were okay.

He began to speak. "Well, I wish I could tell you . . ."

No, no, this is not happening. This was not supposed to happen. This was not supposed to be possible. I remember little of what else was said, for this is when the panic ensued. My mind began to panic.

". . . but I have some bad news."

Dr. Burch went on to talk about what might have happened, but I wasn't listening. I was drowning. He was speaking through a wall of water, or he might as well have been.

When he paused for a breath I blurted, "Should I have called Friday? Could you have saved her?"

"No, I don't think it would have made a difference."

Suddenly I realized he hadn't said what the bad news was. Or at least I hadn't heard it. My mind fought to the surface of the water, gasping for air, grasping at hope. Maybe it was bad but she could still be saved. Maybe, oh, maybe . . .

"What is the bad news, exactly?" I hesitantly asked.

Please say it's not as bad as I think. Please say there's a problem but it's fixable. This can be fixed. Please.

"Well, I don't see a heartbeat."

Again, irrationality prevailed. *Okay, he still hasn't said she's gone. He hasn't said she's dead. How are we going to get her a heartbeat again? How are we going to fix this?*

"Do you mean she's gone?"

"She's gone."

My back arched up off of the table. It is done. She is gone. I am finished. There was no more air. I was sinking deep, deep down into the blackness. The flames licked against my legs.

But God came close. My Father, my God, hemmed me in.

I began to shake again. I longed to weep, to melt this despair in an explosion of violent tears, washing away all the darkness, all the pain. But no tears would come. No refreshing, cleansing tears. I was frozen. I was hardened. I was stone. The nurse, with tears spilling down her cheeks, hastily handed me a handful of tissues and embraced me. But I couldn't cry. *This is not fair*, I thought to myself. *This nurse can cry, but I cannot shed one tear for my baby girl.*

Dr. Burch wrapped his arms around me. "I am so sorry. I am so very, very sorry. Are you here alone?"

Yes, I am alone. So alone. But he is here.

"We'll call Brian, and when he gets here, we'll talk about what needs to happen next."

Brian arrived a few minutes later. I will never, ever forget that moment when he walked in the door. A fresh wave of pain crashed over me as I realized who else would be affected by this loss. I was not alone. This was not just my grief to carry.

The thoughts pounded inside my mind: *Oh, my husband. I have failed. I have failed to keep your only baby girl safe. I have failed you. I have failed my boys. I have failed to safely carry the baby sister they were ecstatic to meet, to care for, to protect. I have failed us all.*

We went to Dr. Burch's office, and he discussed again the likely causes of death. He emphasized that we would be tempted to place blame, but he told us with unyielding authority not to do so. He repeatedly told me that it was not my fault, that there was nothing that could have been done. He discussed decisions we would have to make—burial, funeral options, and so on.

And God was there.

I know he was there because he spoke through Dr. Burch. In our initial self-protective shock reflex, Brian and I both felt that we didn't want to see our daughter. But Dr. Burch insisted that we would need to grieve this as a loss of a family member. I listened patiently to him, but the words seemed empty, and they didn't seem to apply to me. In the end, he was so very right. How thankful I am for his God-given wisdom and direction in those first hours.

Then Dr. Burch prayed. My obstetrician prayed for us. He took our hands and cried out to God for us: two shell-shocked people who were barely keeping a hold on reality, who were brain-stem breathing at that moment. I don't remember much of that prayer, but I distinctly remember he prayed that we would have "the peace that passeth under-standing" and that we would still "praise God" through it all. I remember at the time finding that so very strange. I wasn't angry with him for praying it; I felt no instinctive rebellion against it. I just remember thinking they were such very strange phrases to include in prayer in this moment.

Looking back now, after all that has transpired over the past many months, I can see that his bold prayer was answered on both accounts. There has been both praise and peace. And it has made all the difference. Oh, Holy Spirit of God, how you amaze me.

It was decided that we would deliver Anna later that afternoon.

When we left the office, it was snowing. My chills started again. I got in Brian's car and called my mother. My father answered. I was immediately tongue-tied. How do you tell your father that his first granddaughter has died?

I asked him, "Are you sitting down, Dad? I think you need to sit down." I paused. No way to say it except just to say it. "Dad, we lost the baby. She's gone."

I remember clearly he said, "Oh, Honey, oh, Honey." Over and over. "Oh, Honey, oh, Honey." What else could he say? What else was there to say?

And then came one of the most haunting sounds I'd ever heard in my life. I heard my mother wailing. Terrible, wailing sobs like I've never heard uttered before.

I had planned to ask them to come up to Nashville to take care of the boys while Brian and I were in the hospital delivering Anna. I only now realized the enormity of what I was asking them to do. I was asking them to postpone their own grieving to come and happily care for my two young sons. My brain scrambled for any other alternative but could find none. Someone we knew well and trusted was going to have to care for our sons. I was methodical, robotic, taking care of details with precision and responsibility.

I spoke clearly with my Dad. "We have to be at the hospital at two o'clock to begin the induction. Can you come this afternoon to take care of the boys tonight?" He assured me they would pack their bags and be on their way immediately.

Then, as I sat there shivering, waiting for Brian to come back to the car after gathering my belongings from work, I realized that it was our wedding anniversary. Our stillborn baby girl would be delivered on my seventh wedding anniversary.

Dr. Burch had given us the option to induce the following day, December 7, but I wouldn't hear of it. I had carried a dead baby in my stomach all weekend, and I just wanted it out. I wanted this heavy burden of death out of the pit of my belly as soon as possible. Also, I couldn't imagine what we'd do the rest of the day if we weren't immediately induced.

We drove home and began making phone calls. I called our friend and sitter, Molly, and asked her to pick the boys up from school and keep them until my parents could arrive. I told her what had happened. Later she would tell me that my voice sounded eerily calm, as if I were describing a situation that was happening to someone else. Even as I spoke, I realized I wasn't the one speaking. Some force was carrying me through these hours, helping me to arrange the details that had to be arranged. Molly cried while I spoke (again, *she* cried and I could not). I realized that this loss would be hard on her as well. I was asking a great deal of her in asking her to be completely calm so that we could explain everything to the boys ourselves. But she bravely agreed that she could do that, out of her great love for me.

Brian then called his parents. I got on the phone a few minutes into the conversation and his mother was sobbing, saying over and over again, "I am so sorry. I am so sorry." Brian's father lovingly offered us a burial plot that he'd secured some time ago, though we ended up declining his generous offer.

My next phone call in those eerie few hours before the induction was to our friends Eric and Jennifer. They had suffered a late miscarriage just a few months prior to our loss, and we were feeling overwhelmed by the sheer number of different decisions we were facing. For us they were a living example of what the apostle Paul said in 2 Corinthians 1:4, "[God] comforts us in all our troubles, so that we can comfort those in any trouble with the comfort we ourselves receive from God".

After the phone calls, I wandered listlessly around the house. I re-packed my hospital bag, angrily pulling out all the cute clothes I'd packed for my first girl to wear during her hospital stay. At the last second, I decided to keep in the suitcase the dress I'd chosen as her "coming home outfit."

I look back on that now and know God was there. He guided my hands as I saved that dress. It now hangs in my room, along with a beautiful picture of Anna wearing it for her memorial service, stained ever so faintly by her precious blood.

Brian and I barely spoke to each other as we roamed the house, waiting for the minutes to pass. As I thought more about the boys and how they would find out the news, I realized we needed to just tell them ourselves, and we needed to do it right then. Dr. Burch had told us that it would be wise to seek counsel in the way we told our boys about the loss. He stressed that there was a right way and a wrong way to tell children about this kind of thing. I was terrified of damaging my sons for life with this first close experience with death. But I hadn't been able to reach a counselor by phone that day. I prayed to God to give us the words. I knew in my heart that he would guide us. He was there.

We went to pick the boys up early from school. On our way, I called Molly to let her know that Brian and I were picking the boys up from school ourselves, and Brian and I discussed what we would say and who would say it. Brian asked to be the one to break the news to them, and to this day I am grateful for the godly man who took it on his shoulders to be the leader of our home that day. We had a supernatural calmness as we greeted the boys. They didn't ask one question about why they were leaving early and why we were both there to pick them up. It was an uncharacter-istically quiet drive home.

Once we arrived at home, my oldest son Camden started looking sad. I believe he was picking up on the fact that bad news was coming, although when Brian asked him what was wrong, he said he was sad because it wasn't snow-ing at our house as it had been at school.

I sat down in our armchair and Brian sat in front of me on the ottoman. Brian pulled Scott, our three-year-old, into his lap. I seated Camden next to me, snuggled up into my side, and wrapped my arm around him. Brian began.

"You know how we've talked about heaven? About how people go there when they've stopped living?" Brian told the boys that we had been to the doctor and that Anna was not going to be able to come home with us. He explained she would never live with us here on this earth, but that she was going to go straight to heaven. He told them that heaven is a wonderful place and that God and Jesus were going to take good care of her for us. He told them that we would get to meet Anna when we get to heaven."

I had once heard a speaker say, "The biggest difference between a Christian and a non-Christian should be our response to death, our attitude toward death. This is what can change the world." That comment had been engraved deep into my soul. I knew it was imperative that my boys' first encounter with death not be shrouded in fear and hope-lessness. With all that is in me, I wanted my boys to view the death of this earthly body as victory. I wanted them to live the truth of 1 Corinthians 15:54, "When the perishable puts on the imperishable, and the mortal puts on immortality, then shall come to pass the saying that is written: 'Death has been swallowed up in victory.'" I wanted to clothe them with God's impenetrable armor, so that Satan would never be able to use the grief of unexpected death as a weapon to pull them from the arms of their God. I knew that this was my first chance to teach them that trust, true trust in God, is a shield no matter what the circumstances.

And so together we told the boys, "It is okay to be sad. We are going to be sad sometimes and might even cry. But it is also okay to be happy that Anna already gets to go to heaven. We don't have to be afraid of dying, because we know that if we love God, we get to go to heaven. No matter what, we need to trust God. Always trust God."

Camden put his head down and cried, disappointment etched across his face. Scott had no outward reaction. But, oh, how these boys have talked about their sister! How they have prayed for God to keep her safe in heaven! How they have talked about her laughing with Jesus! They have drawn picture after picture of Anna and God and Jesus.

We would later learn that we had done everything, *everything*, exactly right in breaking the news to our boys. Counseling materials told us that it was important to speak openly, to speak of death with finality (as opposed to some mysterious disappearance), to be in close physical contact while telling them. He was there. Guiding our hands, guiding our tongues.

We told the boys that Nana and Papa were going to come and stay with them while Mommy and Daddy went to the hospital, and their little resilient hearts were again bursting with joy. I told Camden that Nana might be a little sad and might cry, but Camden said proudly, "Well, I'm not going to cry, because I've already been sad."

My parents arrived a few minutes later. They were so strong for the boys. Mom said they tried to get most of their crying done on the two-hour drive here so that they could be strong for the boys. I talked to Dad a few minutes about what we knew so far and what decisions we'd made and were facing. I told him we'd been advised not to have an autopsy, and he agreed that in his experience in hospital administration autopsies were generally discouraged. He gave me several hugs. I will always be in awe of the way my parents were able to hide from the boys their own grief for not only Anna but for me as well, and have fun playing with them for several days. God was not just providing for me. His arms of love and provision were wrapping around my entire family.

Brian and I drove in almost total silence to Baptist Hospital. As we pulled into the parking garage, I thought, "This is not what I imagined it would be like, coming here to this hospital." The parking garage was very full. We finally found a spot and made our way inside. The woman at the check-in desk didn't look up at us but gruffly asked, "Are you here to deliver?"

"Yes."

"Are you in labor, or is it scheduled?"

How to answer? Yes, I was actually in early labor. Dr. Burch had discovered I was dilated to two centimeters and was having bloody show as well as good contractions. I was beginning to get uncomfortable. Yes, it was "scheduled," but only a couple of hours ago. And no, I hadn't in fact scheduled to deliver a dead baby today. I hadn't really planned for any of this to happen. I finally answered, "Yes, I think it's scheduled."

She didn't react to this odd statement. Without ever looking up at us, she asked us to sit down and wait. This was certainly not the compassionate greeting we had hoped for. I cannot describe the burden that had settled around me, on top of me. I sat in silence, uncomfortable, dejected. I still wasn't crying; I believe reality was still slowly settling in. But it was such a dreadful feeling, sitting there waiting to be checked in so I could deliver a dead baby.

When we were finally called back to the desk and I told a different woman my name, she said, "Oh, we've been waiting for you." She quickly gathered up forms and took us back to our labor and delivery room immediately. "We don't want you to have to sit out there and fill out all these forms," she said. For that, for this first taste of compassion here, I was thankful.

As we walked the long stark hall to our room, we were told that a man had been there already, looking for us. She described him. We later found out it was our friend Eric. We'd asked him not to come, but he knew firsthand our heartache and came anyway, willing just to sit in the hall and pray if we couldn't bear to have company. This was the first inkling we had of what all was going on at that very moment outside of us, outside of those hospital walls. How the army of God's people was amassing—our extended family, our friends, our church family—and was mobilizing to help carry our burdens, to hold us together when we threatened to crumble. We were trying to keep quiet, to keep alone, to shoulder this cross ourselves, but the Spirit was working in the hearts of God's people despite our efforts. We would not carry this burden alone.

Once in the room, I was left to change into a hospital gown and wait for a nurse. I was freezing even in bulky clothing, so I trembled again as I made my way to the hospital bed in the sparse gown. Rita, our nurse for the afternoon, came in. She said she didn't know who our nurse was supposed to be yet, but she was just going to come in and help get things started until they figured out the schedule. She ended up volunteering to stay with us, and God showed his compassion again. She told us of her mother's history of recurrent miscarriage, and I realized my pain was a pain with which she was well acquainted. She spoke of her abiding faith in a loving God. She patiently answered our questions about the options for Anna's burial. She quickly got me the things I asked for—ice chips, warm blankets, the epidural. She sought out a referral to the chaplain on call, even though we were undecided about that service and didn't ask for it ourselves. She took care of Brian, giving him his food and drink options while he waited. I cannot imagine a better nurse for those first few hours of our time there. It was obvious she was experienced with this situation, yet it wasn't just routine for her. On a day when I'm sure she would have preferred to assist in a healthy, happy birth, she chose to labor with us and to minister to us. Again, God provided.

I passed those early hours of labor with my Bible. I meditated on the verse from Psalms: "The LORD is close to the brokenhearted" (34:18 ESV). I said it over and over and over and over again. Slowly, relentlessly, I began to feel its truth. It is difficult for me to describe just how close he began to feel in that time and space. I felt so much grief, yet so much confidence. Unyielding sorrow mixed with unyielding peace. Warmth returned, slowly but steadily. Light started to replace the darkness. I believe with all my heart that the very presence of God slowly rolled into that small hospital room and swelled until it filled every inch. There, in that quiet room, he began the work of healing my broken heart, even as the medical staff attended to my pregnancy. I believe he sobbed with me as he gingerly, gently picked up the shards of my shattered heart and began to knit them back together with the skillful precision only my Maker's hands could possess. I would later know for certain that he'd not just repaired a broken heart, but that he'd imbued it with a new strength, a new resilience I'd never known before.

The labor progressed more slowly than I expected for a third child. We passed the time quietly. I read the Psalms intermittently, prayed for my boys intermittently. People came and went—nurses, the doctor, chaplains—but mostly it was very quiet. At some point, reality started to set in, and at a random and unexpected time in the afternoon, I finally began to sob. I am sure to an outsider it would seem as if that was the high point of my grief, when the tears built to a crescendo. However, to me, that was when I finally started to feel some comfort. It was comforting to let those tears wash over me, to know I hadn't become a hardened, hollow shell of a person. I sobbed for about thirty minutes, I suppose, during which no words at all were spoken. I was simply allowed to sob.

Eventually, it was time to push. Many have asked me about that, about the difficulty of enduring the physical demands of labor, knowing the child would be born dead. Thankfully, my body just went into autopilot. This was my third child, so my body had done this twice before. Once it came time to push, I just concentrated on pushing the right way. Thankfully, Anna was born quickly.

I had asked the doctor to take a good look at our baby first before giving her to us. I mistakenly thought I might decide not to look at her, not to hold her. I didn't think I could stand it if she was badly disfigured, if it was obvious from the disfiguration that she had suffered in death. I didn't think I could stand to see physical evidence of her suffering. Dr. Burch needed to examine her anyway to see if there were any obvious indications of the cause of death. When he had finished his short examination, he told us there were no obvious indicators. There was no sign of umbilical cord strangulation or cord problems of any kind, all of which had ranked high on the list of possible causes of sudden fetal death. He assured us that she did not look disfigured, that he really thought we would want to see her.

Oh, how the tears poured as he placed my baby girl in my arms. She looked so perfect, so beautiful, so peaceful, just as if she were sleeping. It took several seconds to see any sign of death at all—the only one being that her topmost layer of skin was peeling and blistered in just a few places, though not on her face at all. Her eyes were rimmed with the faintest blue shadow. Her lips were the most beautiful deep red I have ever seen. She looked as if at any moment she might open her eyes and look at us. To me, she looked like the perfect mix of her brothers' best features; Brian whispered that she looked just like me. We were so proud of her. The bond and the pride were instantaneous, just as they had been when my two living sons were first placed in my arms. Though tinged with a sadness and pain, that moment, that first moment, was otherwise exactly the same. I hadn't expected that.

We spent the next four hours holding Anna, rocking her, putting our fingers in hers, kissing her, and talking to her. We spoke of how much we loved her, how very much we would miss her, and of what her life would have been like here with us. We essentially talked through a lifetime with her—how her brothers would have made her laugh, how her daddy would have taught her to ride her bike and how to garden. We told her how she would have been my shopping partner and chick-flick movie partner, how her brothers would have scared off any potential boyfriends. We made a lifetime of memories with her in our minds during those four hours, and it was so joyful. Four hours of pure joy, while we wept heartbreaking tears.

The next morning a few family members arrived. We tried to keep most people away; this grief felt too personal and private. We wrongly thought that our families had no attachment to Anna as yet; we thought they would only be sad for us. We were so wrong on this account, and we realized it as soon as we brought Anna into the room with them.

Again, the moment was not as I expected. At the same time, I felt such sorrow and mild guilt for putting them through this, for not keeping their granddaughter safe inside me. But I also felt deep pride and joy as they marveled over her, as they kissed her cool cheeks and cradled her close. So many, many tears and so many, many smiles all blended together. God was with us, wrapping his arms around us, weeping with us, while also surely smiling at the happy, living Anna with him in heaven. So many paradoxes.

We will never know for sure what caused Anna's death. But it is quite possible that Anna's death saved my life.

December 8, 2010

My Dear Sweet Anna,

How I long to hold you in my arms, kiss your sweet cheeks, see your smile, and hear your laugh. You have forever changed me. You have given me so many precious gifts without ever having drawn one breath on this earth. What can I give to you?

My precious daughter, I will give you these:

- I will bear this ache, this pain of missing you, so that you will never have to know pain in any form. You will only ever know the life that God intended—perfection, joy, light, eternity—in his arms.
- I will make your name and your memory known. You will forever be a part of this family.
- I will do my best to help your brothers, your father, and me get to heaven so that we can be reunited some day. So that we can be together for eternity, never to be separated again.
- I will carry some part of you, some remembrance of you, with me always.
- I will record in this book, to the best of my remembrance, my short time with you physically, and will record how you have changed us all.

A Quiet Moment:
"Do You Trust Me?"

Trust in the LORD with all your heart, and lean not on your own understanding. In all your ways acknowledge him, and he will make straight your paths. —Prov. 3:5–6 ESV

This is the first scripture my boys ever memorized. I can think of no better words that I want seared deep, deep, deep down into their hearts and minds. I believe these words will serve my boys well through whatever challenges their lives hold—including, God forbid, the loss of their mother.

My father once told a Bible class, "The whole of the Bible comes down to this: God is saying, 'Do you trust me?' That is the point and question of all of Scripture. Do you trust me?"

When God gave Adam the garden, he asked, "Do you trust me to provide for your needs and trust that I'm right when I ask you to stay away from the one tree?" Adam failed, and blessings were lost.

God asked Abraham, "Do you trust me? Enough to follow me to a strange land? Do you trust me to give you a son when it no longer seems possible? Do you trust me enough to give me back the son of promise? Abraham did, and, oh, how God directed his steps and showered blessings.

"Do you trust me?" God asked Ruth. He asked Esther. He asked David. He asked Job. And he showed himself to be ever faithful when they trusted him alone.

Jesus asked, "Do you trust me, trust the Father, enough to live differently? Do you trust that God knows what is best for your life?"

The Bible is a blessed account of how God has proven time and time again, in both individual lives and in dealing with huge nations, that he can be trusted and is the *only* thing to be trusted.

So this is my life's desire: to trust. And in these days, the second phrase of Proverbs 3:5–6 has taken on new meaning: "lean not on your own understanding." There are many, many things about suffering, especially my own, which I do not understand. But that's okay. It is actually a relief to me that I do not have to understand; I do not have to figure out the great cosmic meaning of human suffering.

God only asks me to trust and to acknowledge him in all my ways. That's not a Sunday-morning-only kind of action. "All my ways" is an all-encompassing phrase, indicating a God-centered, God-filled life. Do you trust me, Sara? Enough to acknowledge me in *all your ways*: in laundry, in school drop-off, in treating patients, in serving your husband, in cooking dinner, in sitting in chemo treatment rooms, in illness? This is the life I seek.

And then we come to the ending, the blessed, beautiful promise: ". . . and he will make straight your paths." Yes, my Father, that's what I need. I need you to direct my paths. That's what you've proven you'll do time and time again: for Abraham, for Israel, for Ruth, for Esther, for David, for so many.

Prayer

Heavenly Father,

I would not have chosen this schooling. Am I that difficult to teach? And am I this slow at learning? But, Lord, you have proven time and time again that you know just what you are doing with time. Thank you for bringing me to a point of daily and full dependence on you, and when I am healed, I ask that I not lose that sense of utter dependence. I continue to beg for your mercy. I ask that in your mercy, in spite of the fact that I don't deserve it, that you will remove this cancer fully and completely, and that you will grant me the miracle of another baby girl; a child whose very existence will be a tangible reminder of your power and love. Those are my heart's longings, so I lay them at your feet.

Lord God, I trust that your plan is perfect, no matter what it is and whether I like it or not.

King Jesus, seated at God's right hand, I ask everything in your *name*, which I love above all names.

Amen

A Family Prayer

On December 4, 2011, Sara and her family and friends held a balloon-release ceremony in honor of Anna. This is the prayer her father Jody Pigg prayed at the event.

Dearest Heavenly Father, the giver, sustainer, and exalter of life and all that is good,

The great I AM . . . the true and only God . . . We lift our hands, hearts, and hopes to you this day in our remembrance and celebration of our children, the ones here with us today, and especially the ones now with You.

We beg you to come to us. Send your Spirit, your angels, your heavenly hosts to us. Come deep into the secret, sacred chambers of our thoughts, where we hurt, hunger, and are most tender from the aches and sorrows of loss and longings.

Oh, God, layer your holy truths on our emotional scars . . . whisper to us those soothing words of Jesus, "Do not let your heart be troubled; do not be afraid . . . in my Father's house are many mansions. . . . It is true; let there be no doubt. I am here, and so is Anna, your precious child. You, too, are my precious child, and there is a place for you here with us as well . . . where we can be together forever."

Oh, God Almighty, send us your peace . . . hold us close and give us rest.

And brighten our today with the precious promises of eternal joy, wonder, energy, and excitement that await us on the great day when we all soar through the heavens, meeting our Lord in the air.

Quicken our steps in childlike, joyous anticipation for the day we are whisked away to the home prepared by a loving Father for his long-awaited children, with the shouting and rejoicing of angels and heavenly beings on the day we are reunited with those we love and long for so deeply.

Lift us up high this day, Father; bless our remembrances of our children, renew our spirit, and send us soaring through the heavens. . . . Reunite us now in faith and hope while we wait . . . and keep us clothed, warm, and secure in your everlasting love.

Through the perfect Son, Jesus Christ, we, the "born again," cry out to you this day.

Amen

Chapter Two

Diagnosis

Exactly four weeks after delivering Anna, Sara started feeling excruciating pain high in her abdomen and to the right. The pain came like a bolt from the blue. There was no buildup, no twinges of pain, just sudden, gut-wrenching agony.

She went to the emergency room, and the medical staff went to work on her. When the doctors looked at her chest x-rays, they noticed something odd. They weren't looking at Sara's liver—not intentionally, anyway—but part of Sara's liver happened to be in the frame of the x-ray, and it didn't look right. Upon further investigation, they realized that Sara's liver was full of metastasized cancer—cancer that had spread from somewhere else in her body.

After extensive tests, Sara's doctors finally reached a diagnosis: Stage IV colon cancer. It was pretty close to a worst-case scenario. Surgery wasn't an option; so much cancer was in Sara's liver that almost no liver would be left if they removed the malignancy. Radiation was impractical for similar reasons.

It was a medical mystery, much the way Anna's death had been a medical mystery. There had been no previous symptoms. No family history. No other risk factors. Sara just went directly from healthy to terminal. Do not pass Go. Do not collect $200.

Another sort of person might have questioned God's goodness. Another sort of person might have felt abandoned. Another sort of person might have wondered why she was being punished. Sara, however, saw things through her own unique perspective. Instead of retreating into a cave of self-pity and anger, Sara started reaching out, ministering to other people through her words.

Exactly one week after her diagnosis, she started a blog on Caring Bridge that would soon impact thousands of people's lives. The first words of her first entry in many ways encapsulated everything she would write through the rest of her days:

> In awe. Overwhelmed. Thankful. Fearful. So
> many, many emotions competing within me
> these days. Thank you all for reminding me of
> God's power and his goodness.

Sara opened herself up to the world and said, "Here I am." She was honest about her conflicting feelings. And as she lived in her reality, she discovered that her reality was a good place to live. Yes, there was fear. Yes, there was sadness. But even in the midst of all that, there was great thankfulness in Sara's life, and as she leaned into that thankfulness, she found more things to be thankful for. And God became more real to her in the process.

That was one of the things that caused people to be so drawn to Sara's blog. As they witnessed her gratitude, her courage, her faith, they saw the truth of the gospel in a way that a hundred sermons couldn't accomplish.

Far from feeling abandoned, Sara felt, more than ever before, that she was surrounded and upheld by love. Her eyes were opened to a truth that had been there all along: believers are the Body of Christ. They belong to one another. Sara knew these truths; she could quote the relevant Bible verses. But they all felt a little truer when they became a matter of life and death.

> I know we all have trials in our lives. Jesus told us we'd have trouble, right? I hope that you are as encouraged as me by the vast connections throughout this world that being a Christian brings. As my dad put it yesterday, I am simply the current subject matter being discussed in a vast "network" that already existed. If this many people can come together to pray for me, it can happen for anyone.

Sara was a part of a huge divine conspiracy. God had a plan that would change Sara. And it would change a lot of other people too. There would be ups in the journey ahead, and there would be downs. There would be days when Sara would have to admit that she was completely at a loss to understand what God was up to. But even then, God used her honesty to encourage Sara's readers and draw them to himself.

In that same blog post, just a week and half after her diagnosis, Sara turned her attention to Exodus 33. In this chapter, God has told Moses that he is ready to withdraw his presence from the stiff-necked and disobedient Israelites. But Moses pleads with God to change his mind. And God does change his mind—or, more properly, he relents and answers Moses' prayer. Why? Because, God says, "I am pleased with you and I know you by name" (Exod. 33:17). Sara wrote, "This is one of the *main* reasons I get so excited about so many people all over the world praying for me by name. Surely, surely, God knows my name now! Thank you for bringing my name before the Father so much."

Sara was a prayer warrior. She was ready and willing to say, "Not my will but thine," but first she put her own desires into words. In other words, though she said, "Thy will be done," she didn't skip over the "here's my will" part. She loved that image of a God who relents—who pursues a different course—because of the prayer of one who is on intimate terms with him. In the end, her prayers for bodily healing, and the prayers lifted up on her behalf by thousands of people around the world, were swallowed up by God's different and better plan. But, in the process, Sara and all her readers learned just how important it is to be in the hands of a God who says, "I am pleased with you and I know you by name."

Sara started chemotherapy on the first day of February, a week and a half after her diagnosis. Each week, she spent a few hours in the infusion clinic, then she took home an infusion pump that would keep the chemo coming for another forty-eight hours. She was given steroids to counteract some of the nastier side effects of the chemo. For that, her readers were thankful: the steroids made her jittery and wakeful, which made her more able (and more eager) to write. Further into each week, the chemo-induced nausea overtook the steroid-induced energy, so for a while Sara was on a pretty regular cycle of ups and downs.

Sara was a fierce competitor. In high school she had been a standout softball and basketball player. So when she started treatment, she approached it with a competitive spirit. "I was totally *not afraid* today," she wrote on the day she started chemo. "I was fired up. . . . I was ready to, as my sweet friend Kat said, 'Start kicking cancer's booty!'"

This positive attitude spilled over into every area of Sara's life as she reflected on the good things God was doing in the midst of her pain and fear. Her "boys"—husband Brian and sons Scott and Camden—were a particular source of hope and joy.

> As I talk about Brian, I'll try not to gush, but
> I can't promise not to cry. . . . It may not be as
> evident because he doesn't pour out his heart
> *ad nauseum* like I do, but that man is made of
> the strongest stuff there is. Many of you ask me,
> "How's Brian doing?" My answer, always, is, "He
> seems to be doing just fine." And when I ask
> him, that's what he says: "As long as you're okay,
> I'm okay." But that's not really accurate. Because,
> when I'm not okay, he's still strong. He reminds
> me of all the reasons for hope. And I never have
> to do that for him. He is working extremely hard
> right now because, you see, this is his busiest/
> hardest time of year at work right now (Jan.–
> Mar.). But he comes home at 8 P.M. with a smile
> on his face and plays hard with our boys, since

I haven't been able to be really active with them. He is just tireless. He gets up early in the morning and finishes up work, or pays bills, or stays up-to-date on our insurance coverage, until the boys get up and he helps them go potty, find some breakfast, etc., if I'm still in bed, which is often the case. He prays with me and for me at night, and they are the most beautiful prayers I have ever heard. (Now, I'm crying.) He is my rock and my treasure, and he is just about near perfect in my book.

Sara's sons were always a source of humor and hope in her blog posts:

The boys are doing great also. They understand that Mommy is sick and they have to be gentle with me right now, especially with my "button" giving me medicine to feel better. I showed it all to them yesterday and explained that the machine was sending medicine inside me and that it was going to help me not be sick anymore. I explained that we had to be careful with the machine and the tubing. They paid close attention but then were back to their normal, playing selves when we were done. My sweet Scott is fascinated by the port, and he frequently comes and gently pulls my pajamas over just enough to check on it. He looks intently at it for several seconds, then smiles at me. I ask him if it looks okay. He says, yes, and I tell him, "Thank you for checking it for me." They said the sweetest prayers for me last night. Camden prayed, "Please

help Mommy's medicine to work and make her
not sick anymore." Scott prayed after Camden
and said, "Please help Mommy's . . . medicine to
not choke her and to make her feel good." Guess
he saw some potential for strangulation with the
long tubing. And, as I tried to sleep last night, I
figured he just may be right!

As Sara's readership grew, so did her prayer coverage.
Her words blessed people, and they sought to bless her back
through prayer and encouragement. One reader organized
a day of group fasting and prayer on Sara's behalf, and readers from at least eight states participated. Another reader
wrote to tell Sara that she was committed to fasting weekly
on Sara's behalf.

"They all strengthen my soul," Sara wrote of the many
people praying for her, "and I think they all are very deadly
to the dark forces."

Nevertheless, Sara had to face the facts that she had a
deadly disease and that it was very possible that God's plan
was not to grant the bodily healing that she and so many
people longed for and prayed for. The idea that she might
die was something she couldn't commit to writing in that
first spring after her diagnosis. But even so, she knew that
the answer was the presence of God.

Here, in the night, I've been reminded that I
might . . .
Oh, I can say it. I can think it. But I'm not
going to finish the sentence for the sake of my
family who will read.

45

Here, in the darkness, my faith wavers, my hope wavers, the fear threatens.

I will choose to look at Jesus. (Just typing the name, I feel its power.) When Peter walked on the water, during the storm, to Jesus, he started to sink only once he began to look about him at the waves crashing around him. I will reach for Jesus and cling to him. At times, it is with white knuckles. At times, I have to repeat his name over and over in my head and wait to feel in my heart that he is present. But I choose in this moment, in the darkness, to stop looking at the storm about me and to look at my Savior.

". . . Let us also lay aside every weight, and sin which clings so closely, and let us run with endurance the race that is set before us, looking to Jesus, the founder and perfecter of faith" (Heb. 12:1–2 ESV).

Fix our eyes on Jesus. . . . In the life of Sara Walker, fixing her eyes on Jesus wasn't just an abstraction or a nice idea. When sickness and death surrounded her like the roiling sea, fixing her eyes on Jesus kept Sara afloat just as surely as it kept Peter from sinking. And keeping her eyes on Jesus allowed the writer Sara to understand that she wasn't the author of her own life. She prayed to her Author,

My Father,

You are the author of my faith, and of the story of my life—write it well. I know how *I* want *this* chapter to end. I know that *I* want my story to be a *long* one, with many, many chapters after this one. But God, I will not skip ahead in

46

my mind. I cannot write this story myself. I will
trust that *you* are the perfect writer, your ways
are higher, and you will work everything out for
the *good*. I will read one word, one sentence, one
page at a time by living one step, one hour, one
day at a time. And I will try to keep my eyes on
your Son. *Help* me keep my eyes there. Be the *perfecter* of my faith. Make it more perfect.

I love you.
In the name of Jesus,
Amen

How exactly did Sara's habit of looking to Jesus play
out in real time? One good example happened between
the third and fourth rounds of chemotherapy. Pulling out a
chunk of hair in the shower is sort of a rite of passage for a
chemo patient, and it can be especially unsettling. For Sara,
that unsettling moment was an opportunity to turn her eyes
upon Jesus—an opportunity to have her faith perfected. She
wrote, "I pulled out a big chunk of hair in the shower the
other day, and that was emotional. But then I took a deep
breath and asked God to prepare me, to help me remember
that it's just hair."

As that first course of chemo was coming to an end, Sara
was praying a bold prayer—the same prayer she had been
praying from the start. "God, work a miracle. Eradicate *all*
of the cancerous cells."

I've been reading back through the stories of
healing in the New Testament. Can't really find
an example of Jesus or his apostles saying, "No,
you don't need to be healed yet. You need to go

through this for a few more months before I show compassion." Sure, Jesus had to put off a couple of people for a few days, but then the healing was full and complete. If the fullness of God is in me, if the same Holy Spirit who raised Christ from the dead is in me, then why not? Why not?

In March, Sara had a CT scan to see how effective that first course of chemotherapy had been. While she waited for the results of the scan, she reflected on the incredible ways God had already answered her prayers:

God has already done so much in my life that I never could have dreamed possible. Why did I, a little, shy, part-time physical therapist and full-time mom, get to talk about God on the Nashville news? Why has this website been viewed so many hundreds of thousands of times? Why is God changing hearts through this story? I can't fully explain it, but I believe he will continue to amaze us all by what he is doing. . . . So I wait in "hopeful anticipation."

And then it struck her: she had a disease that was characterized by rapid growth and uncontrollable spread of abnormal cells. At that point, as she waited for those scan results, she couldn't be sure whether or not the cancer had grown rapidly or spread uncontrollably. But she didn't need a scan to see that something else was spreading beyond control:

Do you know what I see all around me? I see the uncontrolled spread of joy, of hope. I hear people praying everywhere, and I am witnessing rapid growth of spirituality as the prayers become bolder, more heartfelt, rawer, more focused. I see you Christians being abnormal, living your lives more intentionally, savoring the "small" blessings that each day holds.

I beg you, don't let it stop. Don't let the toxic chemotherapy of the world around you kill this rapidly spreading joy, hope, and peace. Let hope metastasize from you, all around you—spreading from person to person as you live your life in bold *joy*, bold *celebration*!

Do you know that that is what God wants for your life? *Hope*, *peace*, *joy*. That is what he created us to know, to feel. I praise God for this season of my life where he has made me know it.

When the scan results came back, it did look as if God had chosen to answer *Yes* to Sara's prayer and the prayers of so many others. Her test results described "significant interval improvement in hepatic and nodal metastatic disease." All the areas of the cancer were reduced. By every indication, things were getting better. The cancer wasn't gone, but things seemed to be headed in the right direction.

There was much rejoicing among Sara's family and friends. But as everyone who loved Sara would soon learn, the real blessing in all this would not be that God gave Sara the physical healing she prayed for. The good medical news would soon be replaced by bad medical news. But the best news in Sara's life had nothing to do with her medical condition, good or bad. The best news was God's presence in the midst of suffering just as surely as in the midst of celebration. Sara was learning to be still, to know that God was God no matter the circumstances she found herself in.

Before that brief respite of good medical news—while the medical news was still very much uncertain—Sara wrote a meditation that expresses how deeply she embraced the presence of God in the midst of her struggle:

> One night, in the days after Anna's death, as we were putting the boys to bed, I realized that I may never have another baby to cuddle and hold. I then realized that my boys will very soon be big enough that physical contact from old Mom will be "yucky," so I asked Scott, my three-year-old, for a "special snuggle" in his bed. I crawled in bed next to him and held him close, talked about his day, and just enjoyed spending a few quiet moments with him. Ever since then, every night he asks either Brian or me, often each of us, "Can you peas snuggle wif me?" Well, because we are acutely aware of how fleeting this stage will be, we typically oblige.
>
> So last night, I crawled into Scott's bed for a snuggle. He'd had a big day, and well, he was just in rare form. He was past the point of tired, to the delirious point. He was rolling around all over the place and talking a blue streak. Seriously, I couldn't get a word in edgewise, and I couldn't get him to calm down enough to relax and get to sleep. He'd had a few meltdowns in the evening, and I *knew* he needed to relax and have a good

night's sleep. That's what his little body needed. But he would not allow himself to get still enough to let that happen.

Finally, I say slowly and emphatically, "Scott. *Be. Still.*"

I laid one arm over him, lovingly, gently, but firmly enough to stabilize him and help him to calm down and get to sleep. I held him close. He didn't fight it. He just curled into my arm and very quickly fell asleep.

As I lay there listening to his even breathing, I thought, *Oh God, is* this *what you're doing for me?*

I got the distinct picture of God lovingly, gently, wrapping his arm around me to *stabilize* me and "force" (for lack of a better word) me to relax and see the beauty of the life that I was missing.

He hasn't dumped heavy burdens on top of me to pin me down into a contorted, painful position where I'm forced to look at him and plead for release.

He's used loss, cancer, and chemotherapy-induced fatigue to put me into a position of stillness. And while there, he's wrapped his arms around me to stabilize me. I can feel his love in that embrace, just as I know Scott felt it in mine.

See, I was drowning. I was missing *life-filled moments, pure joy moments* all around me in my endless quest for that mythical perfect day. You know, that day when my to-do list was all crossed off, when everything in my house was in its perfect place, when every square inch of this house was clean and organized to within an inch of its life. As much as I was longing for my baby girl, I was overwhelmed with the thought of adding one more child to fall miserably short of perfection in raising. One more child to feel guilty about neglecting while I cleaned and cooked and frantically crossed-off my to-do list. I felt like I was drowning just with two children. In my hurry-scurry pace I was "rolling around all over the place and talking a blue streak"—to myself, to God, to anyone who would listen, with my "woe is me" diatribe.

I am ashamed. I am ashamed that it took all of this tragedy for God to get my attention.

So he whispers to me, "Be still and know that I am God." "Trust me."

Not, "Be still with your body but then work your mind furiously in prayer to say just the right words so that you can get what you want."

Not, "Be still and I will tell you all the answers you desperately want."

Not, "Be still just long enough to read your Bible with an air of self-righteousness so that you can mark it off your list of good things to do and then move on to the next item."

Not, "Be still and doubt the fact that the *fullness* of God dwells in you, because that doesn't make any sense."

He said, "Be still and *know* that I am God" (Ps. 46:10, emphasis mine).

"Be still before the LORD and wait patiently for him" (Ps. 37:70).

"The LORD will fight for you; you need only to be still" (Exod. 14:14).

"The Levites calmed all the people, saying, 'Be still, for this is a holy day'" (Neh. 8:11).

"Be still before the LORD, all mankind, because he has roused himself from his holy dwelling" (Zech. 2:13)

"He got up, rebuked the wind and said to the waves, 'Quiet! Be still!'" (Mark 4:39).

Not sure, but it sure seems like there's something to this idea of stillness. I'm having to learn the hard way what true stillness is. God has had to gently and lovingly "pin me down" to calm me down, to calm my inner storm. I hope it doesn't take that for you. I hope we can all practice this: just being still with God, physically and mentally, even if just for five minutes. Just crawling into his lap and feeling his love, his goodness, without having to say or hear (read) a word. Just resting in his arms. Trusting that *he is*, he is who he says he is, he *always* is, and that's enough.

Maybe soon we can say as David did: "Surely I have calmed and quieted my soul; like a weaned child with its mother, like a weaned child is my soul within me" (Ps. 131:2 ESV).

A Quiet Moment:
Why Me, God?

Why was I born to two loving, faithful Christian parents whose tremendous love for each other is only eclipsed by their unyielding love for you? Why me?

Why was I born into a prosperous, free nation and have never known hunger or neglect? Why me? Why, why was I blessed to attend Christian schools throughout my secondary, college, and graduate education, being nurtured by dedicated Christian professors and making lifelong Christian friends who have challenged my faith and helped me to grow closer to you? Why me?

Why, why did you give me success in school, so that I never struggled to eventually grasp difficult concepts and make the grades needed to enter my professional career? Why me?

Why did you give me a Christian husband who has fulfilled every dream I've ever had about the man I would spend my life with—who is faithful, patient, hardworking, even-tempered, nonmaterialistic, handy, smart, and a fun but teaching Daddy? Why me?

Why did you give me a job right out of school with amazing Christian co-workers who have become dear friends, and enjoyable patients to treat, and for a family-based company with its priorities straight? Why me?

Why God, why did you give me not one but two beautiful healthy boys with no physical or mental disabilities or limitations? Boys who bring me such pride, joy, and laughter each day? Why me?

Why Father, why did you let my dreams come true in being able to stay home with those boys some days and also be able to serve patients a few days per week? Why did you work it out so that they were always being taken care of by Christian friends in their homes while I was working? Why me?

Why, Lord, have you placed me in a city with multiple top-rated medical institutions full of brilliant and also caring medical professionals? Why me?

Why, my sweet Father, have you walked with me every day of this journey? I've been asking the wrong questions. These are where I try to direct my mind now. These are the only why questions I have a right to ask.

Lord Jesus, hold me in your arms. No, better yet, bring my face just inches from yours, gently cradle each side of my jaw, and fix my eyes on you. Keep them there. In your strong gentleness, do not let me turn my head even one fraction of a degree to the left or right, to see the wind or the waves. I want only to gaze at you. You are real. All else is passing away. You are real and true.

Prayer

My Father,

I am in awe of your love for me. I am in awe that you care so deeply for this brief whisper of a life here in this fallen world. You have already given me everything. You gave me Jesus. You freely gave me an eternity sharing in Christ's inheritance, which I have no claim to whatsoever.

You gave me your Spirit, so that I am never alone. So that I can know a peace through this dark world that defies explanation.

How can I ask for more? And yet I have. I have asked that you stretch out your mighty hand and heal this dying body, for a little while longer. I have begged for your mercy and compassion, to allow me to help my husband and raise my sons. You know I long to see you face to face. You know I long for it as I have never longed before. But you also know my love for those boys, a love that you planted in my heart.

God, make me fully well and, in so doing, make your name great. Remind us of your incomparable power; cause us to tremble in fear for a moment again, before we realize with great thanksgiving that you are for us, your chosen people.

God, who am I that you should show me such love? I love you, my Father. I trust that all your ways are good and right, and are too wonderful for me to understand. I rest in your wisdom and perfection, your perfect love. I treasure you today, Father.

Amen

Chapter Three

New Sara

Jesus had a habit of answering questions that people didn't even know they were asking. When Nicodemus caught up with Jesus one night, Nicodemus thought he would soften up the famous teacher with a well-turned compliment: "Rabbi, we know that you are a teacher come from God, for no one can do these signs that you do unless God is with him."

Jesus, however, wasn't there for small talk. He got right to it: "Truly, truly, I say to you, unless one is born again he cannot see the kingdom of God." Nicodemus was confused—and who can blame him? But Jesus didn't let him off the hook. "Do not marvel that I said to you, 'You must be born again.' The wind blows where it wishes, and you hear its sound, but you do not know where it comes from or where it goes. So it is with everyone who is born of the Spirit" (John 3 ESV).

Sara was a little girl the first time she was born again. But her thirty-third birthday, she believed, marked another sort of rebirth, and that rebirth was at least as mysterious as her first one. The wind blows where it wishes. So does the Spirit. And on the day Sara's diagnosis was confirmed, the Spirit moved in a way that no one could have guessed. Sara's terminal diagnosis didn't strike new fears in her heart. No, through that diagnosis, the Holy Spirit freed her from old fears that had always held her back. On her blog she wrote:

> As for my birthday, well, New Sara was born that day. That day, along with the experience with Anna, of course, my vision became clearer. God rescued me from all the worries about things that just don't matter in this world. God helped me to see more clearly his power, his presence.

That was January 20, 2011. Exactly one week later, Sara started her Caring Bridge blog. In one sense, that's not a surprising thing. Lots of people with serious medical conditions keep their friends and family updated via Caring Bridge. But for Sara, more than that was at stake. She had always been a writer. As a little girl, her words flowed like water, exuberantly and joyfully. When she wrote, she felt God's pleasure. But like so many people, along the way she lost touch with her deepest gifts. In spite of the encouragement of her family, her teachers, and her friends, she lost confidence in her talents. It's the curse of so many young writers: as children they write unselfconsciously, celebrating the mere fact that they can shape sentences and stories out of midair. If they compare their writing to anything, they compare it to the nothingness that came before it. Before, there was no story, but now there is! As they grow, they begin to realize that some writing is better than other writing. The more they set their sights on that better writing, the more they're aware that they aren't there yet. And for perfectionists like Sara, that gap between where they are and where they want to be is the open door through which fear and discouragement enter. So for Sara, it was truly an act of faith to start her blog.

As she wrote in that first blog entry, "My God is big enough to handle my fears, and he asks me to lay them at his feet. What I'm still learning is how to leave them there." Through her struggle with cancer, Sara found that she finally had no choice but to leave her fears at the feet of Jesus. And, in so doing, she began at last to live out her calling.

One of the most remarkable things about reading Sara's blogs is watching how her sense of her own identity is transformed through her suffering. She comes to understand what it means to be a child of God and to be known by him the way a child is known by her father.

In her second blog post, she talks about Exodus 33, in which Moses has a hard talk with God. God has ordered Moses to lead the Israelites into battle to possess the land that he has already promised to them. But the Israelites rebel against Moses and God, refusing to fight against what appear to be impossible odds. Not knowing what else to do, Moses simply asks God for his presence: "If your presence will not go with me, do not bring us up from here." Sara focuses on God's answer to Moses: "This very thing that you have spoken I will do, for you have found favor in my sight, and I know you by name" (33:15,17 ESV).

Sara surely felt like Moses. *I don't know what to do next. I only know that I need God's presence.* And God's answer was not only his presence, but his fatherhood. As Sara's

Father, he was pleased with her, and he knew her name; it is the father, after all, who gives a child her name. One of the ironies of Sara's career as a blogger was the fact that while she was getting in touch with her truest self in Christ, the world was coming to know her in a somewhat narrower sense. A year into her illness, Sara wrote, "This is why I feel constrained on [Caring Bridge]. In this place on the World Wide Web, I am defined as 'The Cancer Patient.' I am the young mother with colon cancer. But that is not who I am. I am a child of God temporarily residing in this time in this body until I go to my true home, my forever home. So this body has cancer. So? I'm getting rid of it soon."

Cancer set Sara free because cancer ensured that she would never again let this world define who she was or how she saw herself. The world, she knew, perceived her all wrong. She imagined someone looking at her situation from the outside:

> Oh, that poor woman! Imagine, being thirty-three and being told you have advanced cancer. Imagine the fear of knowing you may not have long to live. Imagine the sadness of looking at your two young sons and thinking you may not get to be around to see them grow up, graduate from school, get married, have kids . . . etc., etc. Imagine that poor man, thinking he may have to raise those two boys by himself.

As Sara admitted, she herself would likely have had the same thoughts if she had seen someone else facing similar circumstances. But she was seeing things from the inside, and it had completely changed her perspective. Her life, she now understood, had always been in God's hands and not hers. "It's not like before I was diagnosed with cancer I had any more guarantee of living to see another day than I did after being diagnosed." Nor, she added, were her "healthier" readers in any different position. "And it's not like any of you without cancer have any guarantee of living longer then me. Sorry, but it's true." Her diagnosis had also freed her to speak her mind bluntly!

But even in her bluntness, Sara wrote to give her readers hope. That really was her specialty.

> When I came face to face with this reality, with my mortality, I realized something. Actually, I don't *have* to die. Jesus did it already, so I don't have to. Actually, this soul is *not* mortal. It's immortal.
>
> "Christ Jesus has destroyed death and has brought life and immortality to light through the gospel" (2 Tim. 1:10).
> *Destroyed death*!
> So what am I afraid of? My soul lives on! It never dies! Sure, this body dies (but I've always had complaints about it anyway). Sure, there's some transition into my next body, and I don't really know how that works, but I'm pretty sure it will be a really cool thing. And my soul doesn't die during that transition.

There's an old catechism from the early days of the Protestant Reformation called the Heidelberg Catechism. Its first question asks, "What is your only comfort in life and death?"[1] The answer is just another way of saying what Sara said:

> That I am not my own, but belong with body and soul, both in life and in death, to my faithful Savior Jesus Christ.
>
> He has fully paid for all my sins with his precious blood and has set me free from all the power of the devil.
>
> He also preserves me in such a way that without the will of my heavenly Father not a hair can fall from my head; indeed, all things must work together for my salvation.
>
> Therefore, by his Holy Spirit he also assures me of eternal life and makes me heartily willing and ready from now on to live for him.

Those whom the Son sets free are free indeed. They are free from the fear of death, because they know that they belong to the Author of life, who works everything for their good, for their salvation. But, just as importantly, they are free from the false and insidious belief that the world can fulfill any of their desires. They are free, in other words, to find joy where joy can be found. For those of us who believe ourselves to be solidly entrenched in *this* life, the things of earth seem very real, very solid.

Brennan Manning's *Ragamuffin Gospel* had a big impact on Sara; she quoted the book more than once in her blogs. A couple of passages from Manning especially highlight how Sara's new understanding of herself as a child of God gave her new freedom—freedom that she extended to her readers: "A little child cannot do a bad coloring," wrote Manning;

"nor can a child of God do bad prayer." It is hard to imagine a sentence that more clearly expresses the freedom that flows from our understanding our true position as children of God. When we offer up our prayers the way a child offers up a coloring to her parent, we can expect the same reception that the child expects: delight and love. These words were balm to a person who had always demanded as much of herself as Sara had.

She continued with a further quotation from *Ragamuffin Gospel*:

> A father is delighted when his little one, leaving off her toys and friends, runs to him and climbs into his arms. As he holds his little one close to him, he cares little whether the child is looking around, her attention flitting from one thing to another, or just settling down to sleep. Essentially the child is choosing to be with her father, confident of the love, the care, the security that is hers in those arms. Our prayer is much like that. We settle down in our Father's arms, in his loving hands . . . essentially we are choosing for this time to remain intimately with our Father, giving ourselves to him, receiving his love and care, letting him enjoy us as he will.[2]

Letting God enjoy us as he will—the idea couldn't have been new to a woman who had grown up in gospel-centered churches and a gospel-centered family, but the Old Sara wasn't yet ready to live in that delight.

The New Sara, on the other hand, reveled in the truth that God delighted in her. And she wanted to make sure her readers knew that God was crazy about them too. Each of her readers, she insisted, was God's favorite, just as she was.

> Good morning, God's favorite! Do you remember that you are? You are a beautiful, perfect, unique masterpiece of the Creator, made to fulfill his special unique purpose for *your* life, made to glorify his name in a way no one else can. How wonderful is that?

And what is the appropriate response to the realization that each of us is God's favorite? Celebration. Joy. Merriment. Sara wrote, "Now, I believe there is a serious place for awe, for reverence, for silence and stillness before God. But it seems that I go to that extreme too often. There is definitely a place for joy and celebration!! We've been liberated! That should excite us!"

In letting herself be delighted as the child of God, Sara got in touch with a new childlikeness. A month after her diagnosis she wrote about enjoying a mud puddle with her boys.

> Today we savored a nice, big, muddy puddle in the back yard. Well, actually I watched them savor it. They splashed and splashed and basically were true to their Pigg genes in looking like a couple of hogs rolling around in the mud. Old Sara would have *never* allowed it. Old Sara would have thought it wasn't worth the massive cleanup afterward. But, oh, how I delighted in their giggles today!

New Sara took the world a lot less seriously—in some ways. In other ways, she took it a lot more seriously. Facing eternity, Sara didn't float off into a vague spirituality. In many ways she got *more* in touch with the physical world God had placed her in—its mud puddles, birds, grass, trees, and little boys.

At the same time, Sara longed for heaven with an urgency that Old Sara knew nothing about.

> My ears strain every moment of the day to hear the trumpet call.
>
> Oh, I've always thought it would be nice to go to heaven someday. It would be a pretty nice place. I'd have a bigger house, and it would be sunny all the time, and I think I will be able to fly, and that's exciting. But at the same time, I've had these thoughts in the past, "Jesus, it would be great if you came back, but I'm really looking forward to this family vacation in the Bahamas next week . . . or . . . I've worked really hard on this first birthday party, can we please have that first . . . or . . . but I really want to see what Stephanie's baby will look like, can you wait until after he's born?" No more. I pray every day for Jesus to come get us. I kinda think it's doubtful that praying for it is going to make it come any quicker, but it just comes out anyway in my prayers.
>
> This world is so full of pain, injustice, suffering. I hurt for myself, of course, but I also hurt for those children starving in Somalia, for those

women and children in abusive relationships, the orphans, the crippled . . . I could go on. My own suffering has opened my eyes to how much suffering is all around me. And I imagine how much it must hurt God, who loves us all more than we can imagine . . .

So I long for him to come and make things right. And I'm thankful for that new longing in my heart.

Sara's longing found its focus in Revelation 21–22, John's vision of the New Heaven and the New Earth, where God will live with his people. "He will wipe every tear from their eyes," writes John. "There will be no more death or mourning or crying or pain, for the old order of things has passed away" (Rev. 21:4). Suffering was teaching her to savor this world, but still she yearned for a world where her suffering would be no more, swallowed up by the presence of the Father who wipes every tear from every eye.

The contrast between the New Sara and the Old Sara of perfectionism and comparison is clearest, perhaps, in the first post of Sara's second blog, *Savoring the Day*. In starting this blog, she was reintroducing herself to the world, not as "that young mom with colon cancer," but as a voice of gospel hope—hope clarified, to be sure, by her struggles with cancer, but not defined by it. She thought carefully about what she wanted this blog to be. More to the point, she thought carefully about what had happened in the heart of the Old Sara when she read the blogs of moms who had it all together, when she browsed the pages of Pinterest, that factory of self-comparison and self-loathing. She wanted a blog that gave readers the kind of freedom that she had experienced herself. "If I accidentally stumble upon another blog of a homeschooling mother of eight," she wrote, "I am going to crawl into a hole. I am going to crawl into a hole and start muttering, 'You is kind. You is smart. You is important.' Over and over and over again, whilst sucking my thumb and twirling my hair."

Sara had a sense of humor. She also had a point. Even the most well-intentioned mom blogs have a way of creating anxiety and doubt and self-flagellation. It's not the bloggers' fault. As the old saying goes, comparison is the thief of joy. The problem is in the reader's heart more than in the blogger's words. So Sara spoke directly to the hearts of her readers—and, free from shame herself, she felt free to be kind even to the bloggers whom Old Sara had compared herself to:

> No offense to you homeschooling moms. No offense to you mothers of eight or more. No offense even to you, homeschooling mother of eight who blogs. Bless your hearts. You are extraordinary.
>
> Bless your hearts, you bloggers with your recipes for organic homemade smoothies with ingredients I've never heard of, and your free printables of "25 Easter crafts to make with your toddlers." I know you mean to encourage. I know you mean to share valuable information that can help us be better mothers. I know it. Deep down I know it.
>
> It is not your fault that you make me want to crawl into a hole. It really isn't. It is not your fault

that I am still sitting over here trying to figure out how you even have time to take a potty break from all the laundry, grocery shopping, and meal preparation that must go along with rearing eight children; much less have a spare minute to take gorgeous pictures of all the crafts and organic goodness taking place in your home at any given point in time. But then write about it in step-by-step detail on your beautiful blog? What am I doing wrong? I don't have the foggiest idea how to even *start* to get to your level.

I have *two* children. One is under the care of the public school system for thirty-five hours per week. One is in private preschool for thirteen hours per week. I am having a red-letter week if we have clean underwear to put on every day and don't run out of bread for school lunches at least once during a two-week span. I wish I was exaggerating.

Does it sound like Sara is being too hard on herself? No, this is Sara celebrating a newfound freedom from perfectionism and comparison. She's so free, in fact, that she feels free to post a picture of her desk in a state of complete dishevelment—the sort of desk that is decidedly absent from Pinterest, *Traditional Home*, and *Southern Living*. She wrote, "Old Sara would not have been able to sleep at night until there were, *at a minimum*, healthy straight little piles. For New Sara, this actually looks tons better than it has for the last couple of weeks because you can actually see some of the desk surface underneath."

There is more than one kind of hospitality. One kind, the kind you see in *Southern Living* magazine, is about creating a beautiful and tidy space into which you can invite guests to relax and enjoy friendship and fellowship. It's a lovely model of hospitality. In that model, however, we sometimes end up missing chances to be hospitable because our houses aren't sufficiently beautiful or tidy or comfortable. There's another model of hospitality that says, "We'll have to shove those unfolded clothes to one end the sofa, but you're welcome to sit there, and all I've got in the refrigerator is half a leftover pizza, but you're welcome to eat it with me. The important thing is that you're here, that we're together."

In her blogs, Sara experimented with that kind of hospitality. Instead of making her online home tidy and beautiful, she invited her readers into the mess, glad they were there. In that first post on the new blog she wrote, "If you are ordinary like me, and this [the disaster of a desk] is more your reality, feel at home here." And here's the thing: by letting go of the goal of creating a beautiful and comfortable space, Sara created a space for her readers that was more beautiful, more comfortable, and more welcoming than she had hoped.

Old Sara had so many fears. New Sara wasn't entirely free of fear, but her fears had changed into something productive. The fears she expressed as she launched her new blog would help ensure that her writing brought freedom to her readers rather than self-condemnation.

Oh, I fear, *fear* that in some way my blog may at some point make someone feel "not _____ enough." You fill in the blank: not holy enough, not spiritual enough, not creative enough, not Bible-knowing enough, not patient enough, etc., etc. I fear that somehow, someway, someone might read something and walk away feeling *not enough*. I fear that if I write about my successes, successes I think you too could achieve, you will not understand that the failings are far more frequent. You will not understand that I truly believe that "If I can do this, if *I* can, I *know* you can do this too. Because I am *so* ordinary."

Sara welcomed her readers because she understood how unreservedly Jesus had welcomed her. Channeling Brennan Manning again, she reassured her readers with the deepest truth of the gospel: "You are enough. You are enough for Jesus. Right now, you are enough. He died for you, for me, in our ugliest, most unworthy states, in our sins."

Sara cared about her readers' hearts much more than she cared about blog traffic. John the Baptist said, "I must decrease, he must increase" (John 3:30 ESV). Sara said more or less the same thing as she launched her new blog:

If you ever come to this place, or any place on the web for that matter, and feel overwhelmed, feel less than worthy—shut it down immediately. Shut it down. Unplug, get up, and move. If you are looking at this blog and you haven't spent five minutes today in the arms of your Creator, just you and him: shut it down. If you are reading my ramblings and you haven't spent five minutes looking into the eyes of your spouse and

listening, *really listening* to how their day went:
shut it down.

Every blogger wants more readers. But to what end?
Sara refused to put the cart before the horse. She would
rather lose a reader than let her blog get in the way of that
reader's walk with Christ. "But I hope you'll hang with me,"
she wrote. "I hope we can figure out this calling together—
this calling to be *in* but not *of* this world. This calling to be
holy as *he is holy*. This calling to take up our crosses."

Sara was a kind of Lady Liberty, welcoming immigrants
from the Old World of self and comparison and perfectionism—immigrants eager to make a new life in another,
better country. She extended an invitation like the other
Lady Liberty's:

> So come to me, all you ordinary. All you huddled
> masses yearning to break free of the "perfect
> Facebook status" and "perfect parent" status. All
> you who have wanted to learn to make smoothies
> for years. All you who are completely befuddled
> by extreme couponing. All you who more often
> than not consider Chick-Fil-A waffle fries an
> acceptable vegetable serving, at least for this night.
> Next week we'll do better.
>
> All you who sometimes fall asleep in prayer.
> All you who have had a New Years' resolution for
> the past four years to read the Bible all the way
> through and fall apart by February. All you who
> have a red-letter day when you only raise your
> voice to your children once.

Paul wrote to the Philippians, "I am sure of this, that he who began a good work in you will bring it to completion at the day of Jesus Christ" (1:6 ESV). If you are in Christ, the "real you" is that completed, perfected work of Christ. He is chipping away at you, and he will finish the job. The New Sara, the one who was born on her thirty-third birthday—was she really new? Or was she simply waking up to the work that Jesus had already been doing in her life?

In April of 2011, just three months after Sara's diagnosis, the first Walker Run was held. Twelve hundred people showed up, and Sara, the New Sara, realized something about her situation that had been true all along.

> The participants began arriving and I was dumb-
> struck. They came from everywhere, and soon
> I looked out and it was a sea of people. I started
> to get weepy. Little Sara, who thought for thirty-
> three years that she was unloved and insignificant,
> looked out over a crowd of twelve hundred
> people, all there to show their abounding love
> and support. I am holding back tears even now.

Sara at that moment was no more loved, no more supported, no more significant than she had ever been. She simply had eyes to see it. And that made all the difference.

In January of 2011, Sara was finally able to throw off everything that had hindered her, the sins of fear and comparison that had entangled her, and she was finally ready to run the race that was set before her. In other words, she was finally able to pursue her calling. In January of 2012, she wrote:

Today is kind of my birthday. New Sara's birthday, that is. One year ago today I came home from the emergency room, having just found out that I most likely had metastatic cancer all over my liver, though we didn't know yet where it had started. I came home convinced I had only hours to live. And in a way I did die that day. Old Sara died. I couldn't have foreseen the events that would take place that would totally change everything about the way I look at life, at relationships, at God. I never imagined I would be writing today words that would be read by thousands of individuals. That God would use our story to strengthen the hearts of his people all over the world. I don't say this to be boastful, except in God. He has done it. All I did was start typing on a website page that my friend set up for me. So "happy birthday to me." I have a new heart, and I am thankful for that.

We can all be thankful for that.

A Quiet Moment:
Unconquerable

Something's a-brewin' inside me . . .

It gets me so fired up that I want to go around shaking people, grasping them by both ears, and then *yelling* in their faces . . . something that makes me literally quiver with excitement and anticipation. . . . Victory is ours! No weapon of Satan can stand against us; there is nothing to fear! The battle belongs to the Lord!

Imagine what it would look like if the people of God stopped cowering in fear, if we stood together, tenaciously proclaiming the victory of God.

Satan, that liar, that great deceiver, who hates us, who hates our families, how he would despise that! How angry it would make him if we dared to realize that we can beat him. Read of God's victories, my friends. Read of them in his powerful Word! He didn't just win. He won *big*, *decidedly*!

Then read of his promises to us. It takes my breath away:

> I pray that the eyes of your heart may be enlightened in order that you may know the hope to which he has called you . . . and his incomparably great power for us who believe. That power is the same as the mighty strength he exerted when he raised Christ from the dead (Eph. 1:18–19).

> Now to him who is able to do immeasurably more that all we ask or imagine, according to his power that is at work within us (Eph. 3:20).

> In all these things we are more than conquerors through him who loves us (Rom. 8:37).

Do you feel unconquerable? Or do you feel defeated? That is a lie of Satan! Are you living victoriously?

Please, please, I beg you, pray this prayer with me. On your knees, hands held high, shout it if you dare. Summon your inner warrior; summon your righteous anger against all the pain, all the fear, all the suffering in this world.

Holy and Great God,

Light a fire inside me. Let it consume me. Consume me with your power. No more, *no more* will I cower in the darkness. No more will I allow Satan to have a foothold in my thoughts. For you have armed me, and I cannot be defeated! Go before me always, and open my eyes to your victory! Today I stand; I stand on your side. Consume your people. I will be courageous.

In the perfect and powerful name of Jesus, who is above all things.

Amen

Prayer

My Heavenly Father,

You never give up on me, and I refuse to give up on you. I know you are wise beyond my understanding. I believe that you are good, that you are love, a deeper love than I could possibly understand based on our weak human version of it, and that you bless those who love you. I do not understand anything about my life right now, but I am thankful you don't ask me to. So instead of thinking about my misery today, I will count my blessings. I will tell you as many things as I possibly can today that I am grateful for: for the sunshine, for my car, that there is gas in it, that

I don't have to worry about my next meal, that I don't have to worry about pain thanks to pills, that my boys are happy in their safe, nurturing schools and that I don't worry about them while they are there, that my husband has a good job and I don't worry about his faithfulness to me or to you when he is away from me.

This is where I will put my mind today.

I love you, God, and I love you, Jesus. To the moon and back a billion quadrillion times.

Amen

Notes

[1]"Heidelberg Catechism," August 17, 2017, https://www.crcna.org/welcome/beliefs/confessions/heidelberg-catechism.

[2]Brennan Manning, *The Ragamuffin Gospel: Good News for the Bedraggled, Beat-Up, and Burnt Out*, Special Anniversary Edition (Colorado Springs, CO: Multnomah Books, 2015), 141-42.

Chapter Four

New Vision

The prophet Elisha once got on the bad side of the king of Aram, Israel's bitter enemy. So the king sent an army to the prophet's hometown to capture him. The next morning, when Elisha's servant went out, he saw the Aramean army surrounding the city. He was understandably terrified. "Oh, no, my lord," he said. "What shall we do?"

Elisha, however, didn't seem concerned. "Don't be afraid," he answered. "Those who are with us are more than those who are with them." It's not hard to imagine the servant looking at the Aramean army, then at Elisha, then at the Aramean army again, and wondering who exactly his master was referring to as "those who are with us." He couldn't see anybody there. Then Elisha started praying: "Open his eyes, Lord, so that he may see" (2 Kings 6:8–17)

When the servant looked again, the scene was very different. The surrounding army, with its horses and chariots, was itself encircled by a vast army of God, with horses and chariots of fire, filling the hills around the city. The troops of Aram suddenly looked puny and ineffectual to the servant who had been so terrified a minute before. Elisha, who obviously had a strong sense of irony, prayed that God would strike the Arameans blind. And that was the end of the siege of Dothan. The people of God could finally see their situation for what it was. The enemies of God were blind and put to rout.

God's people had new vision. They saw something that was truer than their seemingly impossible circumstances. For Elisha's servant, the key moment wasn't a change in his circumstances. The key moment was his seeing and understanding something that was already true about his circumstances: "Those who are with us are greater than those who are with them." The key moment was a change in vision.

From the day Sara's struggle with cancer began, both she and her family realized that much of the struggle would come down to vision—seeing what was truer than seemingly impossible circumstances. One of the first things Sara's father, Jody, told her was to prepare herself for the life-and-death battle for her mind and heart. In a guest post on Sara's blog he wrote,

> Satan is tremendously skilled in prompting our minds to focus on the seemingly insurmountable foes that present themselves during our lifetime. He whispers "give up" . . . "give in" . . . "just let it go." He loves to come to us in the darkness of night, on the dreary days, in the lonely hours, and when we are physically weak. And he is very good at what he does.

Paraphrasing Paul, Jody offered his daughter (and the rest of us) some great advice about how to parry Satan's attacks on mind and heart: 1) take your eyes off the danger before you; 2) reminisce about the many, many times the Almighty God has powerfully intervened and come to your rescue; and 3) give thanks.

That choice—to direct our gaze somewhere besides where Satan would have us look—makes it possible to pray with real focus. "And the certain outcome," as Jody wrote, "is 'the peace that surpasses all understanding' that 'will guard your hearts and minds in Christ Jesus'" (Phil. 4:6–7 ESV).

Jody's words of hope and exhortation for Sara echo throughout her writings for the rest of her life:

> So my precious Sara, fight hard for your mind
> and heart! In this spiritual and physical tug of war
> in which you are now engaged, don't be overcome
> by the view of the powerful enemy that would
> pull you into the abyss before you, but instead,
> ever hold on to the rope of hope. Look over your
> shoulder, and see the powerful armies of God
> who are pulling with you, and let the strength of
> his mighty arms pull you to safety!

We are surrounded by powerful enemies. It's true; there's no use denying it. But here's something that's even truer: those enemies are surrounded by the armies of God. And against those horses and chariots of fire, our enemies cannot stand. The life of faith is a life of learning to see the things that are truer than the things we see with our eyes.

Perhaps Sara thought of the servant of Elisha and his renewed vision when, early in her struggle against cancer, she received a most unusual email from a friend and neighbor. This neighbor described a vision that had come to her as she drove past Sara's house after a prayer meeting.

> As soon as I drove by, I saw another picture in a flash: Your house had the most brilliant light streaming out of it, like there was no roof. Light poured forth all the way up to the heavens and back down. I heard the words, "Now is the time for open heavens in this house." All around giant angels kept bending down, whose heads I could only see when they bent down, and they kept putting these boxes of something into your house. These boxes were brilliantly lit also, and I don't know what was in them. They were gifts of some sort. At times, light particles would fling out of the boxes like sparkler firecrackers. The glory of heaven poured down and faith and praise went up, so just a continual column of light was seen from your house to heaven. . . . Your name is Walker, and that's not by accident. Walk on, woman of God. You are a warrior sent to disperse darkness wherever you go, and that you will do.

What an image! That neighbor saw a truth that went beyond the visible world to the invisible. Sara was like a city besieged by sickness and the threat of death. But the angels of God were giving Sara everything she needed. More than that, they were giving her things she had never had before, equipping her not merely to withstand the siege but to go on the offensive.

Sara—the New Sara—always kept her eyes open for the little hints of God's goodness that the rest of us tend to miss. What do you see when you see a robin? Sara saw the presence of God. Shortly after she started chemotherapy, she noticed a pair of robins that became a recurring theme for the rest of her life:

> There are two beautiful robins that I have now seen at least two or three times a day for the past two or three weeks at minimum. Whenever I look in the yard, either the front yard or the backyard, they are there. They are always in the part of the yard where I happen to be looking.
>
> Yesterday, Mom took the boys to preschool while we went to see the oncologist, and when I returned she said, "When we left the house, there were two robins in the front yard, and I promise they both looked straight at us." I hadn't told my mom about our robins.
>
> A few days ago, when I was pulling out of the driveway to take the boys to school, the robins were parked on our front steps. And I promise you, they held themselves erect, like two watchful sentries.
>
> Two days ago, as we were eating breakfast, I looked out the back doors and saw them both walking along the top of our privacy fence, as if doing their rounds and monitoring the perimeter of our property.
>
> Then this morning, I went to the boys' room to help them find clothes and make up beds. I

looked out the window into the backyard, and
yep, there were our robins. I promise you, they
stopped what they were doing and both looked
straight up to the window. They stared at me in
the window for a good five-to-ten seconds.

So call me crazy, but I think they are my
angels. Or they are at least my visible reminder
that the angels are standing guard. They watch
me, they watch the perimeter of our home. They
stand guard at the front door to my house. And
they are always there. Always on the ground (or
on the fence). Not in the trees or flying around.

The New Sara had a new way of looking at the world,
and she urged her readers to share in that new vision. "Do
you feel like an unbeatable, unstoppable warrior in this
world?" she asked in one blog post. "Do you see with your
eyes of faith the huge angels all around you? If the Spirit
is in you, if you are in Jesus, you are unbeatable! *You are*!
The power of *God* is with you, and his heavenly servants as
well!" That new way of seeing would soon crystallize into
her project of "Savoring the Day," the habit of seeing and
recognizing the blessings that surround all of us every day.

It was as if Sara had stepped through the looking glass,
and everything was upside-down and backward—in the
best possible sense. If you've ever been close to anyone
going through chemotherapy, you know what a miserable
experience it often is. Listen to what Sara had to say during
Round Two of chemotherapy:

It is 1 A.M., and the chemicals which *God* created, which *God* allowed to be discovered, which

God allowed researchers to combine and repeatedly verify their effectiveness against cancer, and which *God* allows caring, compassionate doctors and nurses to administer—also known as chemotherapy—are now coursing through my body. I am doing well so far, actually markedly better than I was on day one of round one. Apparently, one new side effect this time is they have gotten my creative juices flowing. I have lain in bed for the past two and a half hours composing this post, the post that's been "swishing" for several weeks. This is the post I've been hesitant to write for fear that it will lead many to conclude that I am certifiable.

Sara's certifiably crazy idea was that cancer was the best thing that had ever happened to her. Cancer had caused her to come alive, to see the world for the beautiful place it is, to see the truth of God's word. Cancer had given Sara a new lease on life and a new way of looking at things.

Cancer is the most *wonderful* terrible thing that has ever happened to me. Here's God's "foolishness": He's given me such *joy* in the midst of pain. "For the foolishness of God is wiser than human wisdom." (1 Cor. 1:25)

"Take your eyes off the danger," Sara's father had told her. In taking her eyes off the danger, she was able to see things she had never seen before. Cancer was not her master; rather, cancer allowed her to see the things that had mastered her throughout the rest of her life—the fear, the comparison, the urge to control.

You see, I was a slave, and I feel like I've been set free. And I'm so excited about it that I can't keep it in. I've been freed from so many things. I've been freed (at least most of the time) from fear of tomorrow. I've been freed from control: for I cannot cure nor worsen my cancer. It is completely in God's hands. I've been freed from the endless comparisons and ranking I do in my head, the thoughts of: *I'm not talented enough, I'm not smart enough, I'm not good enough at my job, I'm not skinny enough, I'm not as good a decorator as her, I'm not artsy and creative enough with my kids, my house is not clean enough, I'm not as organized as her, I'm not good enough at couponing and saving money, I'm not interesting enough, I'm not fashionable enough. . . .*

Cancer distilled Sara's life down to its essence, and she discovered that the life God gives is good in its essence. The lies of Satan that had concealed and covered over God's gifts vaporized like so many clouds.

I am *free* to enjoy the life I'm living! Life has such a sweetness to it right now! (Oh, it's not sweet all the time. . . . But God is allowing those weak times to be so few and far between that it is truly unbelievable unless you could actually get inside my head and know!)

You see, my vision was clouded, but now I see! And I'm so excited about it that I can't keep quiet. I can't even sleep. Quite literally, a blue sky is more blue. A hug from my boys, from anyone

really, creates a warmer warmth in my bones.
Simply holding hands with my husband is a more
meaningful touch. The laughter of children is a
more beautiful song. The smell of a newborn baby
(this one's really crazy, considering how I miss
Anna) is an even sweeter smell. A long talk with a
friend brings a deeper kinship. My precious parents and siblings, all my family, are more precious
still. My church family feels more like real family.

Near the heart of Christianity is the truth that while
Satan comes to kill and steal and destroy, God always turns
his works of destruction into works of beauty. In other
words, God always makes a fool of Satan. As C. S. Lewis put
it, "Mere Christianity commits every Christian to believ-
ing that 'the devil is (in the long run) an ass.'"[1] If Satan had
hoped that Sara's suffering would cause her to doubt God's
goodness or the truth of his promises, he was sorely disappointed. Sara continues,

> Perhaps most significant, the words of Scripture
> ring truer than they ever have in my life, and
> the presence of God, Jesus, the Holy Spirit, and
> angels are more real (at least most of the time)
> than they've ever been. I can *see* all this now. How
> sad that it took all this suffering to get me here.
>
> So much goodness, so much joy, all around
> me, all the time, and I was missing it.

It is true that some days it would be easier for Sara to
see with her new vision, and some days it would be harder.
Her feelings, like everyone's feelings, went up and down. But

her feelings didn't control her. Her attitude was an act of the will—an act of setting her feelings against the spiritual facts that she knew to be true, and judging in favor of the facts.

> I make a conscious decision every day to hold to what I know in my head, to at least repeat the words of truth even if I don't "feel" their truth. I know God is there. I know he hears. I know he has made glorious promises to his children. I know he loves me beyond my ability to grasp. I know he wins in the end, no matter what.

To know and to feel are two different things. Sara lived in that tension. Every one of us lives in that tension, trying to make that eighteen-inch journey from the head to the heart. Sara let herself feel her feelings. Where she didn't understand, she admitted that she didn't understand. But she came back to what she did know.

> I "feel" abandoned on my dark, uncomfortable days. In hope, I believe he will heal me on this earth, but what I don't understand is the delay, the intense suffering, the escalating suffering. I know the struggle makes me appreciate good days more; I know I am learning dependence upon God, but I don't understand why it has to continue on for this long. Haven't I learned enough by now? Why does it have to be this hard?
>
> I don't "feel" particularly loved at those times. But I "know" that I am.

How did she "know" what she knew? And how did she know it more certainly? As she said, the words of Scripture had come to ring more truly than ever in her life. Sara cut her teeth on Scripture. She had been born on the mission field and raised in the church. When she played make-believe as a little girl, she acted out Bible stories! But the intensity of her experience with cancer brought home the reality that the world of Scripture and the world where we live are one and the same world. The Satan who tormented Job and the God who delivered Job are both as active in this world as they ever were.

A story that Sara told on her blog illustrates how thin had become the veil between the eternal and the mundane.

It was an ordinary moment.

You see, the triggers are often hidden in those ordinary moments. We were riding home from a weekend adventure. My mind was wandering aimlessly, contentedly among a variety of thoughts, not stopping for too long on any one subject but peacefully roaming along a number of different lines of thinking. It had been a good weekend, and we had savored the moments. I was confident of that. The land mine came very unexpectedly.

I was thinking of my good friend, K, who was to be induced into labor the next day. She was to deliver her third child, and my mind began to speculate on the excitement and anticipation she must be feeling on this day. This joyful anticipation of going into the hospital with rounded belly, and coming home with arms full of joy, love, sweet baby smell, and perfect baby feet. Meeting this child she had carried for nine months and beginning the process of discovering all the amazing facets to this new little soul, this brand new creation of the Master Artist.

And without warning my mind flitted to comparison, to what I anticipated from time in the hospital this week. I too was anticipating a long hospital visit, but there was no joy in my anticipation, for I was to prepare my body for another battle with cancer. I would enter with a belly full of disease, a belly not bursting with life ready to unfold, but with dead and dying tissues—necrosis they call it. I would leave with arms empty, and my body holding a little less life-giving blood.

Wasn't it just yesterday that we were eagerly anticipating our Anna? That I was dreaming of our time in the hospital with her, our first meeting—face to face? That I was fantasizing about showing her off to family and friends who came to see us in that happy maternity ward? How did this happen? How did I skip that part? How did I get here again?

The tears burst through, despite my attempt to hold back the tide. I didn't want to add memories of a crying mommy onto the end of a fun weekend full of happy family memories; I didn't want that for my boys. Oh, I let them see me cry from time to time. I want them to know it's perfectly okay to cry out to God, to let him see your emotion, to feel those emotions and still come away knowing you trust him. But not today, let's end this day on a high note. Just today.

Brian: "What's wrong?"

"I just got to thinking about K, I just got to thinking about their baby, about how they are going to the hospital tomorrow and coming home with a baby; and I am going to the hospital this week because I have cancer all over my body." Keep in mind this sentence took several seconds to get out, as I was crying heavily. Bless his heart for piecing it together.

"It's just not fair. Oh, Brian, it's just not fair."

A pause, tears flowing, body shaking, mind grasping for solid ground through this earthquake of emotion . . .

He held my hand and quietly said all there was to say. I'm sure I had just torn open a fresh scar for him, made him feel a pain he had only recently managed to bury. How selfish of me, but how very much impossible to avoid it. He said, "No, it's not fair."

And then a sudden stillness. A sudden sensation of arms wrapped strong around me, a rush of whispered, unintelligible but calming words.

I know this feeling too. Let's talk about unfair.

It was a whisper, the Still, Small Voice.

Understand it was not sarcastic, not condemning, not angry. Just sympathizing truth.

My Jesus, brutally beaten, bleeding, exhausted, gasping for air, because of my sin. Because of your sin. Because of the sin of every human who has lived or who will ever live. Think of every despicable, evil act ever perpetrated on this earth. He carried it all on his back.

He drank the full cup of God's wrath. God's *wrath*: The. Full. Cup.

This man, who was perfect love. This man who was sinless, blameless, perfect. This man who healed, cast out, raised, fed, created, loved. This man who laughed with children and welcomed them on his lap.

This man was brutally tortured, spit upon, murdered so that I can share in his inheritance, so that I do not have to suffer the consequences of my unending selfishness.

And I whine about "unfair."

Let's talk about unfair, my sweet one.

Oh, my Jesus, my loving God,

Surely your patience and your love for me are unfathomable. Be deaf to them, these selfish words of complaint, for I do not want your perfect, loving ears to hear them. I want only to sing praise, to sing my gratitude. Let that be all that you hear. Not because it is sin for me to bring my hurt to you, but because it is not what you deserve. It is not what my heart of hearts longs to bring to you. I want to pour my life out in gratitude, and gratitude alone, to you.

In the name of Jesus,

Amen

"For we do not have a high priest who is unable to sympathize with our weaknesses" (Heb. 4:15).

God took an ordinary moment, and infused an extraordinary truth: "It's not fair." He knows this feeling too.

That's new vision at work. Sara felt her feelings: she felt the unfairness of her situation. But rather than descending into self-pity on the one hand or shaming herself for her feelings, Sara trained her vision on Jesus, who was more real to her than her own feelings.

It is tempting to look at Sara's experience and to say, "It's easy to be spiritual when you have death staring you in the face. It's easy to take the eternal seriously when you know that you might be on the very edge of eternity." Samuel Johnson famously said, "When a man knows he is to be hanged . . . it concentrates the mind wonderfully." Near-death experiences make theologians of us all.

But here's the thing: you are as near death as you have ever been. Tomorrow you will be nearer still. Now is the time to come awake to a new vision. What enemies surround you? Addiction? Materialism? Self-pity? Comparison? Doubt? Whatever enemies surround you, know this: those who are with you are more than those who are with them. The enemies that encircle you are themselves surrounded by the armies of a God who loves you and will never fail to work his purposes in this world. His kingdom comes. May we all have new vision to see it.

A Quiet Moment:
The Best Seat in the House

Imagine someone gives you a free ticket to the Final Four. You aren't sure where your seat is, but you are just excited to be going because your team has made it to the big game! You walk in, hand the attendant your ticket, and he says, "You can sit anywhere you want in the whole arena. Even down on the front row if you want!"

You've had the good fortune to arrive a bit early and there are lots of open seats. You say, "But how will I know if I'm sitting in someone else's seat?"

He answers, "Oh, there are no assigned seats. It is just first come, first served."

So you say, "Awesome! I'm headed up to the nosebleed section. I want to sit pretty far back from the action, where I might get distracted and not be able to see well, much less pay attention."

No? That's not what you'd do? I wouldn't.

But that's what I've done for years at church.

Now imagine this with me: imagine walking into a church service to see the front pews of the auditorium comfortably filled. To see people sitting close together, as close to the action as they can get. To see them talking easily with each other, eagerly anticipating worship. Would you assume that they were all related to each other? That some big family reunion must have gone on in town, and now they've all decided to come to church together?

Guess what—that's what every church service is! We are all related in Christ, and our time of worship is a grand reunion after being out in the world as foreigners, strangers, and aliens.

I've been convicted by a beautiful lady at church who sits in the front row, alone. I've watched as she sits with rapt attention on our minister as he shares the words and thoughts of God. She is so focused, so peaceful, so obviously thrilled to be there and so oblivious to everything else going on around her save her experience of worship to our Father. She nods, says, "Yes; Yes, Jesus," as we sing, as we listen to truth. She truly worships for an audience of one.

And I wonder. What must God think when he enters our place of worship to be with us?

Maybe this is just me. Maybe it's not that big of a deal. But now it is a big deal for me. So my family is going to be trying to move a little closer, down front. Not because we want to be seen, but because we want to show God we are happy to be there. I'd sure be happy if you joined us if you can. But rest assured, I will not judge if you don't. I know there may be many reasons you need to sit near the back. I just want my family to show God that we are excited to be at his table.

Maybe, just maybe, one day our worship services really will start to look like one big family reunion. (And if that day comes, my apologies to the ushers who may miss their jobs!)

Note

[1] C. S. Lewis, *A Preface to "Paradise Lost"* (London: Oxford University Press, 1942, reprint 1996), 94.

Chapter Five

Savoring

New Sara's new vision crystallized into a project that began to take its place at the center of her life-message: Savoring the Day. She came to see everything in her life as a blessing—a blessing to acknowledge and be thankful for, to be sure, but first and foremost, a blessing to be savored. Enjoyment and gratitude are two sides of the same coin. As C. S. Lewis observed, "All enjoyment spontaneously overflows into praise." Lewis went on to say, "I think we delight to praise what we enjoy because the praise not merely expresses but completes the enjoyment; it is its appointed consummation."[1]

The pagan way of savoring is motivated by the philosophy, "Eat, drink, and be merry, for tomorrow we die." That wasn't Sara's kind of savoring. Her new focus on the good things of this world was made possible—and meaningful— by the truth that this world's blessings are just a foretaste of the blessings that will be ours in Christ for all eternity. She could eat, drink, and be merry because she knew that she would never die.

Sara remarked that she was "just now finding it cool that [savor] is so close to 'savior.'" Indeed, it was through savoring that she came to grips with the reality of her Savior's work in her life and through her life. She slowed down—though not, at first, by choice—and found that there were things that were much more important and real than the urgencies that drive us from stressor to stressor. In Sara's lexicon, savoring was just another word for slowing down long enough to see that God was at work.

Sara hoped that her writing would encourage and equip her readers to savor the world the way she was learning to savor it:

> My prayer is that the next time you see a blue
> sky, you will rub your eyes and look again: *savor*
> it and see if it doesn't look bluer. That the next
> time you are faced with either taking care of the
> dishes in the sink or reading the book your child
> just asked you to read, you will let the dishes wait
> until tomorrow, and you will *savor* a snuggle. That
> the next time you are stuck in a long line any-
> where, you will *savor* a chance to let your mind
> wander to praying for someone who needs it.
> That the next time you stay longer than planned
> talking to a good friend and consequently have to
> go through the drive-thru for supper, you will say
> to yourself, "It's okay, I was savoring!" That the
> next time you put your kids in bed fifteen min-
> utes after bedtime because a spontaneous tickle

fight ensued, you will *savor* it. That the next time someone "interrupts" your day to share and trust you with some of the load they are carrying, you will *savor* a chance to be a listening ear and make a difference in that person's life. That the next time you are doing your job, your occupation, to the best of your ability but wonder if you should skimp on it and go home early, you will *savor* the chance to do the job God gave you and do it well, with praise and not guilt. That the next time you have a chance to eat your favorite dessert, you will *savor* it, because God created our taste buds, too! God's goodness comes in many forms that are easily missed!

The word "savor" simply means "to taste." It comes from the Latin word *sapor*, which means "taste" or "seasoning" or "delight." That very same word is the root of the Latin word *sapientia*, which means "wisdom." Think *homo sapiens*, which means "wise man," but also means, in a sense, "man who savors." As Sara understood, true wisdom isn't something that happens in your head so much as in your heart and on your taste buds, and anywhere else your longings express themselves.

The psalmist wrote, "Oh, taste and see that the LORD is good" (34:8 ESV). It is surely no accident that the short journey from head-knowledge to heart-knowledge goes right past the taste buds, where savoring happens. For the eighteenth-century American theologian Jonathan Edwards, knowing God (rather than knowing *about* God) was very much a question of savoring or tasting:

> Thus there is a difference between having an opin-
> ion that God is holy and gracious, and having a
> sense of the loveliness and beauty of that holiness
> and grace. There is a difference between having a
> rational judgment that honey is sweet, and having
> a sense of its sweetness. A man may have the
> former, that knows not how honey tastes; but a
> man can't have the latter unless he has an idea of
> the taste of honey in his mind. So there is a differ-
> ence between believing that a person is beautiful,
> and having a sense of his beauty.[2]

There's no explaining the taste of honey to a person who has
never tasted honey. And all the blog posts in the world can't
really explain God's goodness to a person who doesn't know
how to savor the good life that God has given.

For her own part, Sara warned her very eager readers that there might be lengthy stretches of time when she
wouldn't be updating the blog. Why? Because she would be
too busy savoring her days! Savoring wasn't just a matter
of appreciating the enjoyable things of life for Sara. It was
a matter of seeing the good in everything God put in her
life—including the things we would normally find tedious.
She wrote about savoring housework, for instance:

> This is how I'm trying to approach "normal" tasks
> these days: instead of resenting the laundry, I
> pour into it my love for my family and grateful-
> ness that I have a family to clothe and that God
> has provided clothing. Instead of resenting that
> I have to reorganize the closets again to try to
> find room in this little house for our stuff, I savor

the fact that God has so abundantly blessed us. Instead of hating having to make that second trip to the grocery store because I forgot something, I look to see who in that store needs a nice smile today, and I feel love for my God who makes food so very accessible, who continues to provide our daily needs, and who has granted me another day of life to care for my family.

She went on to quote Brother Lawrence, the seventeenth-century Frenchman who slogged away every day in the kitchen of a Carmelite monastery: "Never tire of doing even the smallest things for God, because He isn't impressed so much with the dimensions of our work, as with the love in which it is done."

On her bad days, Sara savored the moments of relief or pleasure that presented themselves. On her good days, she learned to revel in the normality that she had taken for granted her whole life.

I am most happy to report that my days are gloriously mundane.

Gloriously.

I get up, I eat breakfast and fix breakfast for whoever hasn't eaten yet. I pack lunches, I drive, I go to the grocery store, I pick up toys, I wash clothes, I pick up toys again, I break up wrestling fights that go too far, I clean up spilled milk, I make up beds, I pick up toys, I answer emails, I unload the dishwasher and then immediately fill it back up. I pick up toys, and I go to bed. I stay up too late looking at Pinterest like many of the

rest of you. I pin recipes and crafts that I will
never make.

But here's the amazing thing: the more Sara rejoiced in the
mundane things of *this* world, the clearer was her vision of
the unseen:

> I am falling in love with Jesus.
>
> I want to sit with him, talking to him, listen-
> ing to his word, *all the time*, and I am frankly
> getting impatient for heaven so I can see him.
>
> I thought I loved him before.
>
> I was raised to know him, raised to pray in
> his name. Raised to think of his sacrifice during
> communion. Raised to appreciate his suffering.
>
> But now, now . . . oh, what joy he brings! Oh,
> how I can just see, just *see* him sitting beside me,
> holding my hand, smiling at me. I see him laugh-
> ing a big, boisterous, tear-inducing, belly-shaking
> laugh along with me when my little Scott does
> something funny (which is every day). I imagine
> us in heaven, sitting with our feet dipped in the
> river of life, listening to the birds sing and feeling
> a cool breeze on our faces, talking and just enjoy-
> ing the view. I imagine then noticing the holes
> in his hands and crying, sobbing because he had
> to do that for me, and him wrapping his arms
> around me, wiping away the tears and saying,
> "Oh, Sara. It was my great joy to suffer for you.
> You were so, so worth it."
>
> Sometimes, I stretch my hand out to the side
> and try to hold his hand. I truly do. I know he is

beside me, though these eyes can't see him. I keep
thinking maybe one of these days, for the brief-
est of seconds, he will allow this earthly skin to
feel his own. So far, it hasn't happened. But I keep
my hand there anyway, and just enjoy imagining
it . . . I've never in my life felt that strongly about
Jesus before.

I am falling in love.

Remember Jesus's friends Martha and Mary, the sis-
ters of Lazarus? When Jesus came to visit, Martha bustled
about, cooking, cleaning, and getting the guest bedroom in
order. Mary, on the other hand, was almost no help. All she
wanted was to sit with Jesus while her frazzled sister did all
the work. Martha tattled on her sister: "Lord, don't you care
that my sister has left me to do the work by myself?"

She must have been surprised by Jesus's answer:
"Martha, Martha, you are worried and upset about many
things, but few things are needed—or indeed only one.
Mary has chosen what is better, and it will not be taken
away from her" (Luke 10:41–42).

Sara found that having cancer converted her from a
Martha into a Mary.

Before cancer, I was one hundred percent Martha.
Okay, maybe ninety-five percent Martha and five
percent Mary. A leeeee-tle OCD about cleanliness
and organization, and just *doing* in general.

Now, I just want to sit at his feet. I feel so precious to him. Isn't that crazy? God/Jesus let me
get cancer. They have let me suffer. I never would
have thought that all of this suffering would bring

> me closer to my Savior. But then, of course, it
> has. . . . Who else can I cling to?

"I feel so precious to him," she said. In the midst of her suffering, she knew that she, like the rest of us, was God's favorite.

Knowing that she was the delight of Jesus made it possible for Sara to delight more fully in those she loved the most. One of the clearest signs of her Martha-to-Mary transformation came on that rainy day when her boys found that mud puddle she told about earlier.

Watching children, in fact, became central to Sara's *Savoring the Day* project. She suggested that if anyone were confused about how to savor life, all they needed to do was to watch children, for children are masters at savoring. They marvel at diggers and fire trucks and chocolate milk. They pray with an utter lack of self-consciousness and with no regard to what is probable or possible. They have heard that nothing is impossible with God, and they believe it.

"You know the story about Jesus telling his disciples to let the children come to him?" Sara wrote. "I wonder if it did Jesus, in his human nature, just as much good as it did those kiddoes. I wonder if it didn't lift his burdened spirit." Indeed, why wouldn't it have lifted his spirit?

We can be so forgetful. We are surrounded by a million marvels, yet our attention remains fixed on our screens. Consider the wisdom of Brennan Manning again:

> By and large our world has lost its sense of
> wonder. We have grown up. We no longer catch
> our breath at the sight of a rainbow or the scent
> of a rose.

We get so preoccupied with ourselves, the words we speak, the plans and projects we conceive, that we become immune to the glory of creation. We barely notice the cloud passing over the moon or the dewdrops clinging to the rose petals. We grow complacent and lead practical lives. We miss the experience of awe, reverence, and wonder. . . . How do we live in the presence of the living God? In wonder, amazed by the traces of God all around us.[3]

Children savor because the world hasn't lost its wonder for them the way it has for most adults. "So spend some time with kids," wrote Sara. "Watch them. They will teach us to wonder, to savor. God tells us to have childlike faith. We might as well get ready: heaven will be full of five year olds!"

But how, in day-to-day terms, do we learn to savor this way? Sara had a method she called the "Holy Spirit Agenda." "It has rocked my world," she said. "It has rocked it and rolled it and turned it upside down and inside out. It is the most exciting and unnerving thing I have ever done."

Sara's Holy Spirit Agenda worked like this: every morning, as soon as she got out of bed, she got on her knees and prayed this prayer:

Dear Heavenly Father,

Thank you for another day. Thank you for another day that Camden and Scott have their mother and that Brian has his wife. I will rejoice in this day, for you have made it. Father, help me

to follow the Holy Spirit's leading today and not
follow my own agenda. Help me to follow your
agenda for this day. May the words of my mouth
and the meditations of my heart be pleasing in
your sight today.

Amen

And then the excitement started. Because then she started
to see how God orchestrated her day. "I get to see the beauty
of a God-chosen path," she wrote. "He does choose the most
scenic routes!"

When she began following the Holy Spirit Agenda, Sara
stopped viewing any human encounter as coincidental anymore. She looked through every interaction with "Spirit
eyes" in order to discover which of three possible categories
that interaction fit into:

1) an interaction that God has orchestrated so that I
   may share God's love with that person,
2) an interaction that God has orchestrated so that I
   may receive God's love through that person, or
3) an interaction that will bring about worship
   to God.

Or, to put it in more concise terms, every time she inter-
acted with another person, she asked, is this interaction for
the other person, for me, or for God? "Maybe many of you
have always lived like this," Sara wrote.

Maybe you've purposely made no specific,
minute-by-minute schedule for your day because
you wanted to be open to the Spirit's prodding.
Maybe you often abandon your day's schedule to

do the unexpected service for God, and it never bothers you. Maybe you look at each person you interact with and think, "I need to do something to show the love of Jesus to you." Kudos to you, if so.

That wasn't how I lived in my BC years (Before Cancer). I was a slave to the to-do-list. I had to schedule my day down to the minute if I had any hope of getting everything done that I believed needed to get done. Otherwise, the world would crumple to the ground.

Being out for weeks at a time with cancer treatment pretty much clears up the priorities for a person. The most amazing thing I've witnessed: my world hasn't fallen apart without anyone rigidly adhering to my scheduling and viciously attacking my to-do-list. My mom, my husband, my friends were able to step in to do the key things: provide food, clothing, clean shelter for my family. For everything else, it was okay not to keep such tight reins on everything.

Now we're back to the extras: the soccer, the holidays, the gymnastics, the playdates, the date nights, etc., etc. And I can still keep things rolling while following God's leading for each individual day. God knows what is important and what needs to get done better than I do. If I just have to find time to get the dishwasher unloaded and make that Target return—he gives me that time.

So, what does this look like:

As I said, I start with that prayer. Then I begin to work on whatever it is that I think I should do that day: if it is run an errand or two, I head that direction. If it is work on the ever-present housework, I begin that. If it is a scheduled appointment, I go to that. But I do not ever plan my day down to the minute and hour and specific order of how I will do things. That way, if someone calls and says, "Hey, I think I am going to take the kids to the park after school today; want to come?" I can say, "Yes," and I will know that God wanted me to savor a park afternoon with my kiddoes. If someone comes to my mind that I haven't talked to in a long time and there is no reason for them to come to mind, I take the time to call or text or email them, and usually say a prayer for them as well. If I unexpectedly run into a friend while I'm out, I listen to them in a whole new way, trying to discover if they just need a listening ear, if they just need a hug, if they need me to speak some truth into their life, or if they need something to laugh about. I really listen now.

I do schedule things in advance, of course. I am being asked to speak in more and more settings, and I schedule those in advance. I know this is against the popular women-speak these days, but I try really hard to say, "Yes." Because I trust that God is directing my paths, I try very hard not to say, "No."

Sure, there is a place for discernment in how we spend our time. And we absolutely should say "no" to many things. Things like too much time on Facebook, television, movies, smutty magazines, gossipy phone calls, etc. We are smart people. We know what we need to be saying "no" to. I am convinced it is *not* the "random" human interactions that we should be avoiding.

But I am telling you that my experiment over the last several months now is to try saying "yes" to God's plan, and he hasn't steered me off course yet. He hasn't overbooked me yet. He has planned my time far better than I ever did BC.

I have time to savor lunches with friends who need to feel God's love but also time to organize the boys' summer clothes. I have time to savor baseball in the backyard with my boys but also time to get the grocery shopping in. Do I have time to do my Bible study and keep my house spotless? No, but God knows that the house doesn't need to be perfect. Do I have time to call my grandmother and encourage her and also spend an hour on Pinterest? No, but I have time for a ten-minute scroll through Pinterest because God made bedtime go so smoothly with the boys that I find I have an unexpected free ten minutes just before bed.

So what really is at stake in the Holy Spirit Agenda? Is it really about ten minutes of Pinterest rather than an hour of Pinterest? Of course not. Jesus's parable of the Good Samaritan (Luke 10:25–37) clearly illustrates what is at stake here. A man lay bleeding in the ditch, in desperate need of help, and a priest and a Levite each passed right by. Why? Because they were following their own agenda. They saw a battered man by the side of the road, and apparently they viewed that meeting as coincidental, having no particular meaning to them. But a third man came by, and he held his agenda loosely. He seemed to recognize that there was a reason he and that robbery victim found themselves on the same road at the same time. That third man didn't have the religious pedigree of the priest nor the Levite. His people, the Samaritans, were highly suspect when it came to religious matters. But he somehow understood what the religious professionals didn't understand: the stranger in the ditch was his neighbor, made in the image of God; by serving that stranger/neighbor, the Samaritan served God.

The language of savoring may sound self-indulgent at first, as if the point is greater enjoyment for the one who savors. Enjoyment is an important part of savoring. But savoring doesn't end with the savorer. It awakens the savorer to the world around her or him, and it equips the savorer to move outward with the love of God.

A Quiet Moment:
The Smallest Things

Earlier I shared a phrase with you that I came across a few months ago: "Never tire of doing even the smallest things for God, because he isn't impressed so much with the dimension of our work, as with the love in which it is done." This phrase has spoken volumes to me. You know how I like a well-turned phrase; I thought it might grab your attention if you are anything like me: perfectionist, addicted-to-the-to-do-list, wannabe overachiever, task- and goal-oriented, etc. If you are the stay-at-home mom who wonders if cleaning up children's messes all day is really what you are meant to do. If you are the working-outside-the-home mom who just can't seem to get it all done. If you are a man who feels the pressures of the world on your shoulders.

Chew on that for a bit.

"Never tire of doing even the smallest things for God, because he isn't impressed so much with the dimensions of our work, as with the love in which it is done."

Prayer

My precious Father,

I acknowledge you. I acknowledge you with my head *and* my heart, my words *and* my deeds. I do not understand. I do not understand many, many things. But I am glad that you do, that you know and grasp and understand and *control*. Please direct my steps. I know that you will, for you have promised, and you cannot lie. Thank you for caring for me, little me, oh, Great God of the Universe. Thank you for bending down to guide my steps.

In the name of Jesus, I speak and cry out to you.
Amen

Notes

[1] C. S. Lewis, *Reflections on the Psalms* (New York: Harcourt Brace Jovanovich, 1958), 93-95.

[2] Jonathan Edwards, *Sermons and Discourses, 1730-1733*, Works of Jonathan Edwards Vol. 17, ed. Mark Valeri (New Haven: Yale University Press, 1999), 414.

[3] Manning, 76, 82.

Chapter Six

Prayer

After the "regular" treatments had proven less than a match for her growing cancer, in December 2011, Sara started a clinical trial. It wasn't a last-ditch effort, exactly, but it certainly wouldn't have been necessary if the other treatments had been working. So a lot was at stake.

On the day Sara started the clinical trial, she sat in the doctor's office and the nurse held out a bottle of pills to her. *Wait just a minute,* Sara thought. *Do you realize what you are handing me? Do you realize that to me this feels like my final hope, like you are handing me my cure, what I've prayed about for months? Do you realize the tear-filled prayers that I and countless others have prayed just for me to be sitting here today, being handed these pills?*

She didn't take the pills—not immediately, anyway. She told the nurse, "I just need a minute to pray before I take this." On her Caring Bridge blog, Sara wrote,

And my tears came unbidden. I spoke to the Lord from deep in my heart, as the tears washed over my face.

"Oh, Lord, I thank you for getting me to this point, for making my many lab tests what they needed to be. I need you to make this work. Lord, so many treatments have failed. The cancer has grown, so many side effects have gotten in the way, so much has not gone as doctors expected. Please, not this time. Please have mercy. Please show your compassion. You have worked out difficult details to get me into this study. I believe you led me to it. Lord, let the drugs work. But let my healing be such that it even surprises the doctors. Father, I want you to have the honor and the glory for rescuing your child. Show, without a doubt, that when God is with you, you are different from the rest of the world. You have access to greater power. You are protected in a different way. Show that when many prayers are lifted up, it makes a difference. Give me a chance to tell the story of your great love for me, of when all looked so bleak and the end felt so near, you pulled me up out of the pit. God, please, let this be the beginning of victory."

I wiped my eyes and opened the bottle of pills.

"Are you okay?" the stunned nurse asked.

"I'm okay. I just have a lot of hope right now, and I just really want this to work."

"Well, like I said, we really think this is going
to make you better."

"I know. But I've been told that before. We've
just had a lot of bad happen over the last year. I
really need things to turn around."

There are many striking things about that moment of
prayer in the doctor's office. There was Sara's boldness in
making the nurse wait while she prayed. There was her ear-
nestness and her honesty. There was her pursuit of God's
glory in the midst of a hard, hard moment. But perhaps the
most striking thing about Sara's prayer was the fact that it
came after many, many disappointments. Sara *had* been
praying for healing—earnestly, boldly, diligently—and she
was still as sick as she ever was. Yet she kept on praying.

To read Sara's blog is to be aware of a striking tension. Sara prayed with almost outlandish boldness, fully
expecting a miraculous healing, and she prayed from that
expectation. At the same time, she was fully conscious that
God might have other plans for her. This tension is captured
nicely in two short paragraphs:

> I have spoken recently of my hope, my belief
> that God will heal me. My mind continually
> reverts to the passage in James that states, "the
> prayer of a righteous man is powerful and effec-
> tive" (James 4:16). I know so many very righteous
> people are praying and praying often, and so I
> just can't imagine how God will not hear and
> answer with healing. I have heard such passionate,
> Spirit-driven prayers that I cannot imagine that

God will not act. And as I listen to my kinder-
gartener pray, I cannot imagine how God could
let him down.

And yet I am also very aware of the possibility
that his plan may be for me to die very soon. My
purpose on this earth may be to show others how
to walk into death without fear. Because I do not
fear death. I promise you that I do not. I can state
that with full confidence and honesty.

She wanted to live on in this life (especially for the sake of
Brian and her boys, who needed a wife and a mother), but
she accepted the possibility that her calling at that point in
her life was to die well. How does a person maintain that
tension in his or her prayer life? For Sara, it wasn't always a
matter of maintaining both sides of the tension at one time.
Sometimes she swung from one side ("Let this cup pass
from me") to the other ("Thy will be done"). But she was
honest about that, too.

After one set of bad test results, Sara wrote:

So am I disappointed? Yes. But not devastated.
God continues to show me that I have no control. It is tempting to, and I am probably guilty
of somehow thinking I can manipulate God. My
brain wants to keep some level of control—if
I just believe enough, if I just could pray the
right way, if I could just eat enough broccoli,
spinach, blueberries, and other cancer-fighting
foods, if I could just pray the Scriptures over
myself enough. . . . It is difficult for me and my
oldest-child, perfectionist self to handle not

"winning"—surely it is something I'm not doing right as to why this is not improving faster. This is part of my battle. But as Brian reminded me last night, God has a plan, and it is perfect. I shared with Brian that this is totally rocking what I have always believed about prayer. I know God hears us all, but I don't understand why it seems he will not be moved, not swayed, not act. And yet at the same time, I have seen so many times how he is acting—he is giving me supernatural strength to endure, he has worked out the timing of treatments/scans so that we could take family trips and I could take Camden to his first day of kindergarten yesterday. Through you, he encourages me over and over and over again. Many prayers are being answered. Just not the "big one" yet.

So I must wait. I'm reminded that I am not God. I will thank God that I have today, and I will trust him to take care of tomorrow. I will spend this day watching my children and parents and being thankful for them. I will go to bed tonight and thank God for taking me through this day, and I will ask him to give me tomorrow. I will repeat to myself over and over that I am not alone and that he holds the future.

Living in the tension doesn't mean having everything figured out so much as it means continuing on the journey, remembering "there is only one God, and that God isn't me." Sara never stopped learning. And the more she learned that she wasn't in control, the more she prayed.

One of Sara's many spiritual gifts was the ability to see the truth wherever it presented itself, to hear truth spoken by anyone, even if that person was a little boy. In her last year, when she was in considerable pain, she wrote this lovely piece about her son Scott:

Right now, I'm hoping he's clairvoyant.

My little wild man, the charmer, the heart-stealer, my joy, the comedian, the shoe-lover, the stylish one, the one who teaches me daily what it is to live with a zest for life, what it is to truly savor. I'm hoping we can add prophetic to this list.

We were stretched out on a blanket under the maple tree, he and I. We must have a picnic today, he insisted. It is a sunny day; lunch needs to be enjoyed outside.

Our robins paced on their watchtowers, watchful. Red breasts puffed out in power, in confidence. A gentle breeze licked our cheeks and a slow warmth soaked into our skin. I laid back, linked my fingers behind my neck, supporting my head on bent arms. The familiar strain was immediately present through my upper abdomen.

When, Lord? I am 34, this, just lying on my back, this shouldn't be hard. When will I be able just to lie down again without any discomfort? Something else taken for granted—lying down without pain. How many times did I do this without pain and never thank you? What am I taking for granted now?

And Scott interrupted my thoughts, as he constantly does. As he is doing at this very moment as I type. He cannot breathe without noise. If he is awake, he is making noise. In his room hangs a favorite quote: "boy (n): a noise with dirt on it." He lives this definition; he personifies boyhood.

"Mommy, you have just a tiny bit of cancer."

I opened my eyes, squinting at him in the sunlight. He was only inches from my face. Cheese. He smelled of cheese, peanut butter, and dirt. Always dirt.

It wasn't a question. He stated it as fact.

"Really?" I said.

"Yes, just this much." His index finger tip and thumb were mere centimeters away from each other.

I hope you are right, my son, my wild one. I hope you are right.

I ask to live. Not for myself. I am ready for my eternal home. I long for it. But I grieve to think of leaving them. They are my reason to fight, my will to live. I want to walk through their early years with them, kiss their skinned knees and later their bruised hearts as they face the disappointment that this life eventually brings.

So I beg you to pray. I pray you will beg. *He* can do it. He *can*.

Yes, God *can*. But that's where the tension comes in, isn't it? God can do as he pleases. So why doesn't he please us more, or more often? Sara wrestled with this question. But she never stopped praying.

"I used to be a realist," Sara wrote shortly after starting her *Savoring the Day* blog. "I'm starting to think that was a sin." Many of us are realists when it comes to prayer. We look at the spectrum of likely outcomes for a given situation, and we pray and hope for the most positive of those likely outcomes. And while we're at it, we provide God with a next-best case scenario in case he chooses not to give what we've asked for. Sara wrote,

> See, I used to pray prayers like this: "God, please heal that marriage. But when it fails, Father, please help them not to give up on you." Or like this: "God, please bring full healing to my friend. But when she dies, please comfort her family."
>
> I might mention the miracle in my prayer; I might acknowledge that God had that power. But I didn't really expect him to use it. I expected the logical, the probable outcome. I didn't pray with any boldness. I prayed by giving God an out. That way if it wasn't his will to work the miracle, I was safe. God still answered my prayers. Life was less confusing that way. God was easier to manage, to understand. He fit in my brain, in my realm of logic.

That's an incredible insight. God gave us prayer to stretch us—to expand our inner life out of those habits of control (or, rather, the illusion of control) by which we try to protect the little worlds we make for ourselves. God gave us prayer as a way of ushering us into a bigger reality than what we commonly think of as reality. Prayer reminds us that there's a whole lot more to the world than meets the eye. And yet, as Sara pointed out, there's a way of "praying" that doesn't really get us out of the box of our own making. Sometimes we call out to an invisible God and ask him to work the things of the visible world to our best possible advantage—without otherwise realizing that the "real" world is a whole lot bigger than the visible world.

Sara was at a point in her life where she had no choice but to believe in a God who performs miracles. She freely admitted that. But that didn't make God's miracle-working power any less true.

Sara pointed out that those "realistic" prayers amount to "having the appearance of godliness but denying its power." In case that doesn't sound like a serious matter, consider this list of sins from 2 Timothy 3:2–5: "For people will be lovers of self, lovers of money, proud, arrogant, abusive, disobedient to their parents, ungrateful, unholy, heartless, unappeasable, slanderous, without self-control, brutal, not loving good, treacherous, reckless, swollen with conceit, lovers of pleasure rather than lovers of God, having the appearance of godliness, but denying its power." Those are pretty heavy sins in that list—and there at the climax is "having the appearance of godliness, but denying its power." Reflecting on that passage from 2 Timothy, Sara wrote:

> I don't want to do that anymore. I shudder. I
> shudder to think of how I mentally denied God
> his due power for so many years. So that I could
> understand. So that I could avoid disappointment
> when his will was different. What if I'd had the
> faith to ask for more, to ask for bigger?

Sara continued:

> Jesus says in John: "Very truly, I tell you, who-
> ever believes in me will do the works I have been
> doing, and they will do even greater things than
> these, because I am going to the Father" (14:12).
> What? Greater than healing the lame, the blind,
> the demon-possessed? Greater than raising from
> the dead?
>
> I tend to let the "scope of defeat," the odds,
> determine how I pray. If it is a mild illness, oh,
> then I will pray "bold" prayers for full healing. If
> it is an early marriage problem being handled
> as soon as the slightest hint of trouble arises, I
> ask for full reconciliation. Denying the power
> of godliness?

The scope of defeat—this was a key idea in Sara's way of
praying. To pray according to the scope of defeat is to look at
the challenges we're praying against and adjust our prayers
accordingly. But the size of the challenge is irrelevant, given
the power that is on our side. Early in Sara's illness, when
she was going through test after test to understand what she
was up against, her father told her something life-changing:

> All we are doing right now is sizing up the enemy.
> We are getting a picture of how big he is. But no
> matter what is found, it doesn't hold a candle to
> the limitless power of God that he can unleash if
> he chooses to do so.
>
> It is like tug of war. You are on one side pull-
> ing. All you can see is the vast empty pit in front

of you, and you see the size of the enemy on
the other side pulling you toward it. What you
cannot see with these human eyes, but what you
must fight to see with your spiritual eyes, is the
enormous God and all his heavenly hosts who are
behind you, just over your shoulder, pulling with
you. If you could see them, oh, there would be no
reason to fear at all! You would see you've got this
sewn up. It's not even a contest.

Even Moses from time to time made the mistake of
praying timidly. But God had a penetrating question for
Moses: "Is the Lord's arm too short?" (Num. 11:23). Sara
took that question on as a kind of motto:

> These are my new constant words to God, my
> meditation: Is your arm too short? They remind
> me. They remind me that God *excels* in the hope-
> less realm. That's his favorite place and time to
> work, it would seem. That I have no business
> deciding what is "realistic," what he can and
> can't do.
>
> So, I confess. I was a realist. But now I live in
> *hope*. I am called to have hope, and I am called
> *not* to deny the power of godliness.
>
> I don't want to be a realist anymore.

Even so, we are left with an obvious question: Was God's
arm too short to deliver Sara from cancer? No. His arm
wasn't too short. But he had bigger fish to fry. As the apostle Paul pointed out, "Our struggle is not against flesh and
blood, but against the rulers, against the authorities, against

the powers of this dark world, and against the spiritual forces of evil in the heavenly realms" (Eph. 6:12).

The more Sara's flesh was weakened by cancer, the more she realized that the flesh was never where the action was in the first place. As she wrote to those readers who were so faithful to pray with her,

> I'm a little slow on the uptake sometimes. I don't believe God has given me this disease. I believe he created these bodies to live eternally; that was his original plan. He is the life-giver, the Creator; he hates death. However, because of sin, the wrath of God is also at work in this world. Because of sin, we are vulnerable to the dark forces while in this body. Dark forces have sought my earthly life and have given me this cancer. *That* is what you choose to attack with me, that is what you fight against. I've heard it said that every time a Christian prays, a legion of God's army in the heavenly realms is deployed. I love that picture—that our murmurings to God give an "attack" command to forces in the spiritual world, forces stronger than we can understand. And you choose to ask the Creator of the universe to send his forces to save me. *Wow*. Wow. You *are fighting*.
>
> And this verse also caught my attention: "For in Christ all the fullness of the Deity lives in bodily form, and in Christ you have been brought to fullness. He is the head over every power and authority" (Col. 2:9–10). Did you catch that? Our struggle is against "power and authorities"

and Christ is the "head over every power
and authority."

Can you feel my excitement? My struggle
is not against flesh and blood (wow, do I have
to remind myself of that a lot) but against the
powers and authorities that Jesus is head over.
And I have Jesus. He's come and made his home
with me. Wow, I'm feeling a wee bit powerful today.

And in characteristic Sara Walker style, the
ups and downs of prayer warfare become the
thrills of a roller coaster:

So, as you can tell, we've reached one of the
peaks of the roller coaster. I hope you are enjoying the view.

Here's just a little more for you. Now raise
your hands high and squeal with delight with me
as we take these precious words into our hearts:

"What then shall we say in response to these
things? If God is for us, who can be against
us? . . . Who shall separate us from the love of
Christ? Shall trouble or hardship or persecution
or famine or nakedness or danger or sword? No,
in all these things we are more than conquerors
through him who loved us. For I am convinced
that neither death nor life, neither angels nor
demons, neither the present nor the future, nor
any powers, neither height nor depth, nor anything else in all creation, will be able to separate
us from the love of God that is in Christ Jesus our
Lord" (Rom. 8:35–39).

"I give them eternal life, and they shall never perish; no one will *snatch them out of my hand*. My Father, who has given them to me, is *greater than all*, no one can snatch them out of my Father's hand. I and the Father are one" (John 10:28–30; emphasis mine).

Are you feeling un-snatchable?

Are you feeling like a conqueror?

'Cause ya are!

Are you dizzy yet?

Thanks for strapping in.

A Quiet Moment:
Contentment, Not Comfort

Contentment, not comfort. That is what I am to strive for. Ever-increasing trust in God for daily provisions. He does not promise comfort. But he promises peace, presence. This is what I am learning. Trust. Dependence. Contentment. I am weak, but he is strong. When my world is shaking, heaven stands. When my heart is breaking, I never leave his hands. Never. His hands that shape the world are holding me. He is an immovable Rock that neither slumbers nor sleeps. He does not change like shifting shadows, but is the Father of *light*, who holds me as the apple of his eye. He rejoices over me with singing. He will turn my weeping into dancing. I sow in tears, but I shall reap joy. These are life-giving words.

Prayer

Holy God,

We need you to bring stillness and order back to our minds. We are disoriented, as we are buffeted day and night by the penalties of our sin, and our eyes have trouble fixing on you. Father, I thank you for this time to be with children. For it is really that simple. I want the faith of a child. And so I put my hand in your great big hand, I ask your forgiveness for my tantrums, and I beg for your mercy. I don't deserve it, but in your great love, that's never stopped you before. I love you, my Father.

In the name of Jesus,

Amen

A Quiet Moment:
God Cannot Lie

On Sunday morning, we read a verse that jumped out at me: "'See, I will send my messenger, who will prepare the way before me. Then suddenly the Lord you are seeking will come to his temple; the messenger of the covenant, whom you desire, will come,' says the LORD Almighty" (Mal. 3:1).

It happened just like God said. God sent John the Baptist, and right on his heels came Jesus. He kept his word. *God cannot lie.*

Not one of all the LORD's good promises to Israel failed; every one was fulfilled (Josh. 21:45).

He who is the Glory of Israel does not lie or change his mind (1 Sam. 15:29).

Oh, we can lie to God. Sure we can. We sing, "God will take care of you," when we worship him in song, but do we always believe he is taking care of us? Or we sing, "What have I to dread? What have I to fear? Leaning on the everlasting arms. I have blessed peace with my Lord so near." But do we mean it?

Oh, friends—I have faced the things I feared most! The loss of a child, a diagnosis of cancer. And I testify to this— *God's strength is sufficient*! His burden is light. Jesus bears my burdens, and he lightens my load. He never leaves, never forsakes, never abandons!

God *cannot* lie.

So I cling to these promises:

"Because he loves me," says the LORD, "I will rescue him; I will protect him, for he acknowledges my name. He will call on me, and I will answer him; I will be with him in trouble, I will deliver him and honor him. *With long life I will satisfy him* and show him my salvation." (Ps. 91:14–16; emphasis mine).

Love the LORD, all his saints! The LORD preserves the faithful . . . (Ps. 31:23).

Honor your father and mother—which is the first commandment with a promise—so that it may go well with you and that you may enjoy long life on the earth (Eph. 6:2–3).

God keeps his word. His precious, precious Word. Hallelujah!

Prayer

My Father,

I am overcome with thankfulness for these great days you are giving to me. I rejoice, my soul rejoices in this peace you have poured with reckless abandon into my heart. Thank you for opening my eyes to the tremendous blessings that saturate my life. Help me to remember that I have reason to be bursting with joy every day—no matter the circumstances or challenges that ensue—simply because the great God of the universe is in love with me, makes his home with me, and will be with me forever. Because you go before me, and because you know me more perfectly than all, and yet still delight in me. God, today I don't ask for anything else. I just thank you.

In the name of Jesus,

Amen

Chapter Seven

Transparency

In 2010 before she was diagnosed with cancer, before she lost Anna, Sara was inspired by a Sunday night singing service to write a letter to her church, Brentwood Hills Church of Christ. Her minister read it to the congregation a few Sundays later, keeping Sara's identity a secret. This is what she wrote:

> I want you each to know how deeply moved I was by our last singing service. I'm not sure that I have ever experienced such a sense of true community in worship. It is no secret that Brentwood Hills is blessed to have many members with remarkable singing talent, but last week, there was a deeper loveliness to our typical blend of beautiful voices, and that was the harmony of sincere hearts pouring out our offering to God. The Spirit was moving, I believe. My family, it was a sweet, sweet sound. We were a collection of

broken souls reaching out in hope for the perfection and healing of our God.

As I sang, or should I say *attempted* to sing, through my tears, I was encouraged as I looked around at my spiritual family—many who had eyes closed, or heads bowed, or heads nodding in agreement with the words—singing of their longing to be nearer, still nearer to God. I saw you who have been wounded by recent deaths in your families, you whose hearts have been torn by struggles with infertility or miscarriage, you who have been bruised over and over by battles with addictions yet continue to fight, you who have been beaten down by unfaithful or abusive earthly family members—I saw you earnestly and deliberately sing, "It is well with my soul," and I believed you. I watched you who have bravely battled alongside your children that struggle with disability, you who have chosen to serve the poor, the lonely, the outcast, the difficult to love with your time and your hearts instead of seeking worldly fame and fortune, you who have continued to seek God in the face of burdens, sing, "Lord, reign in me, in my darkest hour," and I was connected to you. We were a group of equals— equally searching and equally longing for our true home.

In scripture, we are called to teach and admonish one another with all wisdom as we sing psalms, hymns, and spiritual songs with gratitude in our hearts to God. My family, you did this, and you do this for me. I was edified; I was encouraged; I was accepted; I was admonished; I was empowered. Praise God for the blessing of corporate worship! Thank you for reminding me that not only are we communing with God in worship, but we commune with each other, as we, in *one voice*, lift our broken hearts to the healer and lover of our souls. Thank you for helping me to truly worship.

Lord God, please don't let us go back to our old ways of polishing up the outside and hiding behind thick walls. Help us to continue to be more and more transparent and *real* with each other! Let us experience that *freedom*!

You've heard the saying, "Be careful what you pray for, because you just might get it." Here was yet another case of that principle at work in Sara's life. After praying for more transparency, more reality, Sara found herself with more opportunities than ever to be transparent and real with a growing number of people. Cancer freed her from the fears that had kept her hiding behind thick walls. It filled her with an urgency that made her impatient with anything short of truth and reality.

"A beautiful thing is happening," she wrote on her Caring Bridge blog.

I can't quite get my head wrapped around it to describe it, but it has something to do with love, transparency, being real, letting our walls down, admitting we don't have it all together, and we are tired of pretending that we do. And, people, it is

freeing! I can see it in your eyes as you talk to me
and feel it in your arms as you wrap me up in a hug,
and I see it among you as I look across the church
building. We are loving each other for the messes
we are, loving without reserve, and it is just exciting.

When she was on her tenth round of chemo, Sara
noticed a nurse giving two women a tour of the treatment
room. It was obviously their first visit to the chemotherapy
clinic. As she was leaving, Sara saw that the older of the two
women was struggling to keep herself together. Old Sara
would have felt sorry for the woman, but she would have
retreated behind her walls and felt sorry for her there. "But
I remembered how dark and scary those first days were,"
she wrote. And she remembered how people had shown
her love. So she went over to the woman, laid a hand on
her back, and asked, "Did you get some bad news today?"

"Yes," the woman said. "It's my husband. It's just a lot
to take in."

Sara told her that the beginning is the hardest. And
then she asked this perfect stranger if she could pray for her.
It was a simple prayer, asking for good news soon, asking
for strength.

"Transparent" literally means allowing light to shine
through, the way a window does. Sara was utterly transparent in the waiting room that day. The love of God that had
shone in her now shone through her into the life of that fearful wife who so badly needed words of hope and comfort.

But there's another layer to that story that is worth
noting. The comfort that Sara gave to the woman in the

waiting room came out of deep and fresh sorrow. The very night before, she had sobbed herself to sleep. And she was transparent about that too. She wrote:

> If God collects all our tears in a bottle, as scripture says, then I'm pretty sure I've filled up enough two-liters to fill a grocery store. My mind had traveled back to about seven months ago, when we were eagerly anticipating the birth of our little girl and there was no heavy burden of cancer. I imagined what I had imagined back then: she would be about six months old, and we would all be enamored of her. I'd be watching my boys hold her and make her laugh; I'd be enjoying learning about girl clothes and figuring out how to keep a little bow or barrette in her sparse hair. Oh, how I wish those days had come to pass.

The New Sara was way past putting on a happy face to cover hidden pain. When she was joyful, she spoke her joy. But when she was fearful or doubtful or depressed, she spoke that too. Why? Because she trusted God enough to believe that he could bring good out of those things and be glorified, just as surely as he could be glorified in our joys and successes.

In May of 2011, after her eighth round of chemo, Sara had a CT scan that revealed mixed results—the kind of results that were to be expected but that were painful to hear nonetheless. She didn't hide her pain. She didn't put on a show for her readers.

I know you've told me I'm inspiring, that I have great faith. But I don't. My faith is so very, very weak. So very, very small. I am so tired and can't find one inspirational thing to say. I have cried an ocean of tears today, over the last several days. I am worn out. I am discouraged. This is what I feel:

> I cried out to God for help;
> I cried out to God to hear me.
> When I was in distress, I sought the Lord;
> at night I stretched out untiring hands
> and my soul refused to be comforted.
> I remembered you, O God, and I groaned;
> I mused, and my spirit grew faint.
>
> You kept my eyes from closing; I was too
> troubled to speak.
> I thought about the former days, the years of
> long ago;
> I remembered my songs in the night.
> My heart mused and my spirit inquired:
> Will the Lord reject forever?
> Will he never show his favor again?
> Has his unfailing love vanished forever?
> Has his promise failed for all time?
> Has God forgotten to be merciful?
> Has he in anger withheld his compassion?
> (Ps. 77:1–9)

So now I go to pick up my boys from school. I will take them out for a special treat to celebrate the last day of school. I will hide my anguish as

best I can and attempt to be happy, to be content,
to trust, to wait. It is such a battle. And I am so
tired of the battle. So very, very tired. But I must
battle, for them, for my precious, precious boys.

"I can't find one inspirational thing to say," she said. And yet the fact that she was willing to tell the truth at all—the fact that she trusted God enough to cry out to him in her distress—was inspiring to thousands of readers.

In many ways, Sara's writings are inspiring the way the psalms of David are inspiring—in their brutal honesty. More than once, friends and readers said they were confused by Sara's blog posts. She would start out talking about how discouraged she was, but by the end, she was praising God for his many mercies.

"Yes, exactly," wrote Sara. "Welcome to the roller coaster. I can go from thoroughly disheartened to overflowing with faith and hope in about two seconds flat." She wrote just like David in the Psalms:

How long, O Lord? Will you forget me forever?
How long will you hide your face from me?
How long must I wrestle with my thoughts
and every day have sorrow in my heart?
How long will my enemy triumph over me?
Look on me and answer, O Lord my God.
Give light to my eyes, or I will sleep in death,
and my enemy will say, "I have overcome him,"
and my foes will rejoice when I fall.
But I trust in your unfailing love;
my heart rejoices in your salvation.

> I will sing the LORD's praise,
>> for he has been good to me (Ps. 13:1–6).

How is that for a mood swing? From "How long, LORD? Will you forget me forever?" to "My heart rejoices in your salvation. I will sing the LORD's praise, for he has been good to me" in six short verses. Sara's comments on this psalm are enlightening:

> Oh, I can just see David wrestling. He knows, has *seen*, God do amazing things in his life. God has delivered him in awe-inspiring, fantastic ways. I'm no scholar, so I don't know when in his life David wrote this psalm, but I imagine it to be after he has killed savage animals with his bare hands while working as a shepherd and after he slew Goliath with just a little rock. He has seen God's power with his own eyes, and he doesn't understand why God is waiting to act now, allowing David's enemy to "triumph over" him.
>
> David wrestles. He wrestles with his emotion. He stubbornly draws his line in the sand, intensely coming back around to what he *knows* in his head about his God.

For David, for Sara—for all of us—there has always been that struggle between what we feel about our situation and what we know about God. As Sara wrote, "David clings to what he knows, while his heart feels abandonment from God. That is where I am. Right there. Thank you, David, for writing this psalm. Thank you, Holy Spirit of God, for inspiring these words. What a comfort they are."

More than once Sara spoke of her emotional life as a roller coaster. "Oh, the exhilarating freedom of the high points!" she wrote.

> I wish I could find the right words to express my joy at "normal days." Days where I can get up and clean up the kitchen, unload the dishwasher, help my boys get dressed and ready for the day, etc. On my good days, I just feel I will burst because my heart is so full. I try to appear "normal" and not about to explode with ecstasy, but if I run into you and I smother you with hugs, I hope you'll understand why. Understand, to me it's like I'm at the top of the roller coaster peak, and I can't help but to raise my arms and squeal.

But if her highs felt unreasonably high, her lows were devastatingly low.

> It's equally hard for me to explain how alone I feel, how desperate for relief, how heavy the burden of cancer is. It feels as if I'm at a playground and everyone else is walking around free, but I am stuck waist-deep in a sandbox, trudging my way around one slow step at a time. I look around at all of you outside of the sandbox and wonder, "Oh, what would it be like to be free, really free of this? To be able to run and jump and skip outside of this heavy sand?" And to be honest, even on my best days it still feels like at least my feet are buried in the sand, for the cancer never really

leaves my mind; it is a burden I can't quite shake
even on the best of days.

There's a lot of pressure to put on a happy face in the
blogosphere—especially on "mom" blogs, and even more
especially on Christian blogs. So, Sara's readers may have
been more than a little surprised to read on Sara's blog,

I think the reason I have not written is because I
have felt completely empty, completely dry, completely abandoned.

Not abandoned by you, but by God.

It takes courage for a Christian woman to admit in writing
that she feels abandoned by God. But Sara was following a
pretty solid example—not just David, who included so many
complaints in his psalms, but also Jesus, who asked, "My
God, my God, why have you forsaken me?" (Matt. 27:46).

Between February and August of 2011, Sara underwent
fourteen rounds of chemotherapy—fourteen cycles of crip-
pling nausea followed by a struggle to get back to some
version of normality for a few days before diving back into
the chemo-induced sickness. Nearly constant were gastro-
intestinal problems, low appetite, and major fatigue, and a
constant back-and-forth to doctors' offices, chemo clinics,
and emergency rooms, punctuated by occasional excruciating pain that sent her back and forth to the emergency
room several times. And through all that suffering, the CT
scans kept showing a "mixed response" to the treatment.
There was occasional good news, but mostly the news on
the medical front was bad. All that suffering, in other words,
seemed to be for naught.

So, if Sara felt abandoned by God, it's not hard to understand why. "This is where I have been, where I find myself on many of my dark days," she wrote in September of 2011, explaining why she had not been updating her blog very frequently.

I have had no energy to write to you from that place, no courage to confess to you my weak, wavering faith.

As my trial continues on, it is becoming harder, emotionally and physically. As my trial continues, I have been distressed to find my resolve weakening, my confidence in God shaking. I do not appear, to myself at least, to be being strengthened by this trial. My faith does not appear to be growing as a result of this testing, but becoming weaker. That embarrasses me. I am ashamed.

A few nights ago, I fell on my face on my floor and cried out to God. "God this is too hard! When, when will you restore hope and joy to this family? Why all this sorrow after sorrow? When will you come to deliver? Why do you wait? I know you hear. Why do you not act?"

That same night, after I got myself together and was able to stop crying, I went to the boys' room, having promised Scott a "snuggle" for a few minutes. Camden asked to join us, so I had one sweet boy on each side of me snuggled up against my side. Camden placed his sweet little hand on top of mine, and they each fell asleep beside me.

It was such a precious, precious moment. God comforted me through my dear little boys.

A month later Sara started a new, experimental treatment. After so much bad news, she desperately needed some good news. What she got was a horrible skin condition—a rare side effect of one of the cancer drugs in her new regimen. She described it as the worst case of acne you could imagine, with hundreds of whiteheads all over her face and neck, behind her ears, inside her ears, and on her chest and upper back. Her scalp was so affected that it hurt to comb her hair.

Sara had already been feeling like Job, but now the resemblance was starting to seem uncanny. Job, too, suffered a skin condition, "from the soles of his feet to the crown of his head"—so bad that he "took a piece of broken pottery and scraped himself with it at his sores while he sat in the ashes" (Job 2:8).

In the Book of Job, Sara found the words for what she was going through:

Why is light given to those in misery, and life to
the bitter of soul, to those who long for death
that does not come, who search for it more than
for hidden treasure, who are filled with gladness
and rejoice when they reach the grave? . . . What
I feared has come upon me; what I dreaded has
happened to me. I have no peace, no quietness, I
have no rest, but only turmoil (3:20–26).

"Oh, that I might have my request, that God
would grant what I hope for, that God would

be willing to crush me, to let loose his hand and cut me off! Then I would still have this consolation—my joy in unrelenting pain—that I had not denied the words of the Holy One. What strength do I have, that I should still hope? What prospects, that I should be patient? Do I have the strength of stone? Is my flesh bronze? Do I have power to help myself, now that success has been driven from me? (6:8–13).

"Boy, do I relate to [Job's] words," Sara wrote. "I have been so emotionally broken over the last few days. I don't want anyone to have to look at my face because it is so grotesque, and so I feel isolated, alone. I have lain in my bed and asked to die. I have begged."

My friends, I type through tears. I do not want to write of giving up, of such overwhelming sorrow. But this is where I am. I can reread your comments, your cards, but all I do right now is hurt. It just hurts. I just don't understand why I must go through such pain. You can't explain it to me. I know in my heart of hearts that God has some plan, and his plan is perfect, but right now I am completely worn out. I don't feel strong enough— I am not made of stone or bronze.

I don't need to be reminded of anything about God, about his Word. I just need someone to sit and cry with me, without saying anything. This is just hard, plain and simple.

My reason to want to live is for my boys, and for my husband. They are the only reasons for

which I cling to life. But I can't be the kind of wife
Brian needs like this—I can't keep the house, nor
meet his needs. I can't be the kind of mother my
boys need like this. Not with this physical pain
and loss of physical strength. I can't play with
them, read to them, bathe them, enjoy them
except in watching from a distance. My heart is
literally breaking into a million pieces as I face
this each day.

Maybe I shouldn't have written today. Maybe
I shouldn't be pouring out this level of despair.

As Sara well knew, any doubts about the appropriate-
ness of her raw honesty were answered by the Bible itself.
She wasn't saying anything that Job or David or even Jesus
hadn't said already in Scripture. Her every reaction, it
seemed, was framed by Scripture. Like Job, she was surrounded by well-meaning people who too often tried to fix
the unfixable instead of just being present with her. Like Job,
that experience caused her to feel more alone on the one
hand, and more reliant on God on the other:

Please don't try to fix me. Please just pray that
God will. Please pray that my skin will heal and
allow me to be out in public again, so that I will
not feel so alone. Please pray, as I know you have
been, that this valley will come to an end soon,
in one way or another. I just don't feel I can take
much more.

In the midst of all this doubt and hurt and sadness,
Sara's father gave her some advice that put everything in

perspective: "Don't let what you don't understand take away from what you do understand." There was so much about her situation, her suffering, that Sara couldn't understand. But she understood that God loved her and had a plan for her that was better than any plans she might have made for herself. She understood that God was God, and that Sara was not.

And just as Job's sufferings gave Sara a framework for talking about her own sufferings, Job's ultimate surrender to God provided a model for Sara's surrender. She felt hurt, she felt doubt, she felt abandonment, but by her own reckoning, she never felt anger toward God.

> I have not, at any point in the last year, been angry with God. Some people cannot understand this, and so I have been trying to formulate an explanation, mostly for myself.
>
> I believe the answer is the fear of God. I have equal parts fear of God and love of God in my heart.
>
> You see, I was raised to know not only the God who welcomes the little children and takes them on his lap, as we see Jesus do; but also the God who came down to Mount Sinai with thunder and lightning and a thick cloud and fire, so that the people trembled and whoever touched the mountain would die. I was raised with the strict instruction to freely approach my Father who loves me more than I could ever comprehend, but *always* to approach him with great humility, realizing his great power and perfect

holiness, with the strict instruction not to ever assume I had him figured out, because he is infinite knowledge and infinitely complex and my finite mind could barely even begin to understand him and his ways.

So who am I to be angry with God? Who am I to question his purposes? This God who loves me completely but who also could strike me down instantly.

When Job asked for answers, God gave Job a vision of himself, and a vision of who Job was before him: "Were you there when I laid the foundation of the earth? Tell me, if you know" (Job 38:4). The answer to our questions, in other words, is not an explanation, but a look at the great I AM. As cancer taught Sara to let go of this life, she had a more complete vision of who God is. And she saw not just a God of power, but a God who gave up his power so that he might die for us:

> And then I think of the cross. I think of how the perfect, loving, sinless Jesus took the full cup of God's wrath, when he deserved not even the smallest sip. He suffered the full measure of God's righteous anger and punishment toward all sin— all murder, all child abuse, all torture, all stealing, etc.—he took it all on his shoulders so that I can live. I think of God's great, incomprehensible love for me in doing this, and I think, *how can I be angry about cancer*? How can I whine about not having a "comfortable life" when this earthly life is just a breath, and he has given me eternal life

in the perfection of heaven? He gave it to me as a free, undeserved gift. The greatest gift I could get. How could I ask for *more*? What a brat!

God is God. I am dust. I am a speck in light of his vastness. What right have I to get angry?

Transparency lets the light shine through. Sara's transparency sometimes looked like doubt. In fact, it was a window to illuminate the deepest truths.

A Quiet Moment:
Why Do You Wait?

A few nights ago, at the end of a very difficult day for me, my four-year-old prayed, "And God, thank you for keeping my baby sister Anna safe in heaven, and thank you for keeping Camden's baby sister Anna safe in heaven." I lost it. I wept. Brian helped the boys to bed, and I fell on my face on my floor and cried out to God. "God, this is too hard!"

A few nights earlier, I had a special God-moment during a conversation with Camden. At bedtime, I had told him I loved him and was proud of him. He said, "I'm proud of you too, Mommy." I asked why and he said, "Because you aren't scared." I was taken aback, not sure what he meant, and he said, "Like that time when I got sand in my eye and it really hurt. I thought I was going to die, and I was scared. But you aren't scared." I haven't talked openly to my boys about not being scared to die. I have no idea where he would have gotten this idea.

Actually, I do.

Because two days before my dear sister-in-law Stephanie had told me, "I know you probably don't want Camden and Scott to remember these hard days, but I pray that they do, that they remember you and Brian and how brave you were through this time."

God showed me within two days how he was answering Steph's prayers.

Prayer

Thank you, Holy Father, for you are truly the lifter of my head.

You continually refresh me with your living water and bread of life. Thank you for this beautiful day, for energy and strength today. Thank you for the way you pour out your love for me in so many ways, including the generosity and thoughtfulness of so many precious, precious friends and family. Pull us all tighter into your embrace today and shine your bright light through us. Thank you, King Jesus.

In your precious and holy name,

Amen

Chapter Eight

The End
Is Not the End

In the fall of 2011, Sara's skin problems eventually began to clear up, and the experimental treatment seemed to be having a positive effect. There were ups and downs, but at Christmastime she was feeling much better, and she was able to enjoy the season with her family.

A February CT scan brought more good news. Sara's cancer had shrunk by thirty-six percent compared to nine weeks earlier, and her family, friends, and blog readers rejoiced with her.

The good news was short-lived, however. The next CT scan, in April of 2012, showed new lesions. Two months after that, a scan showed two small tumors in her brain. Physically speaking, Sara had been on a steady decline for a few months. But spiritually she was stronger than ever. As her father Jody put it, that summer "the hope of physical healing began to fade in the light of eternal glory."

When Sara's friend Molly got the call that Sara had brain tumors, she rushed immediately to the hospital, afraid that Sara was dying, or that at the very least she would need a lot of comforting. Instead, she found Sara in high spirits and lifting the spirits of everyone around her.

A very few days after learning that the cancer had metastasized to her brain, Sara's blog post combined deep peace with a matter-of-fact acknowledgment that she was likely nearing the end of her earthly life:

> God's peace is an amazing thing. I have certainly run the gamut of emotions over the last several days, and still can do so on any given day. I find hope in the fact that the doctors have still not mentioned or speculated on time frames. They have not mentioned hospice care; they have not spoken of end-of-life issues at all. I am trying not to go there ahead of them. . . . I do continue to pray that if God's will is to take me home early, I will go quickly without a lot of deterioration—in weight, in brain function. I do not want my children to remember me like that. So if I go, may it be suddenly.

Sara did everything she could to enjoy her life that summer of 2012. A couple of days after finding out about the brain tumors, she went to the beach with her family. But the car ride from Nashville to Gulf Shores, Alabama, turned out to be seven hours of excruciating back pain. The trip would turn out to be a last hurrah of sorts.

The rest of June and July saw a rapid decline in Sara's health. She had always been a high achiever—captain of her high-school basketball team, chaplain of her college social club, a focused and organized mom. She was smart and driven, often a little too hard on herself. But in the last year of her life—and especially in the summer of 2012—she learned to find freedom in saying, "I need help. I'm not very good at this."

The brain tumors were in her cerebellum, which controls posture, balance, and coordination, among other things. In early July, she began losing her balance and falling down, and she was too weak for the stairs. She started sleeping downstairs on the couch, her husband Brian sleeping nearby on a cot.

And still Sara declined. The brain tumors began to affect her ability to reason and communicate. There were times when she seemed out of touch with reality. In early August, on one of many trips to the emergency room, the ER doctor asked Brian if he was ready for his wife to die. Brian was shocked by the question; the doctor seemed shocked that no one had asked it before. After a short hospital stay in mid-August, Sara came home to hospice care. They had brought a hospital bed into her living room, as well as a walker and a wheelchair. A hospice nurse came every day to help manage her increasing pain. Looking at a family picture on the wall, the home-health nurse asked Brian, "Is that your wife?" To a stranger, the cancer-ravaged Sara in the hospital bed wasn't recognizable as the vibrant Sara of better days.

Little Scott's fifth birthday fell the week after Sara returned home; his birthday party was scheduled for a Chuck E. Cheese's. The family decided to go ahead with the party. Sara by that time was unable either to walk or even to eat, but she was determined not to miss the party. In that last year, she had been even more intentional than usual when it came to making memories with her boys. Friends and family tried to talk her out of going to the party, but she wouldn't hear of it. She had always been determined to fight until her last breath; going to her son's birthday party was another way of striking back at sickness and death. "I'm okay, regardless," she said—that is to say, whether she lived or died—"so let's enjoy this moment."

They had to pull the IV out of her arm, but she made it to the party. She was wheeled into Chuck E. Cheese's in a wheelchair where, free from her deathbed, she watched life swirl around her.

By the time she got home from the party, Sara was exhausted. Brian gathered her frail limbs up and carried her into the house like a baby. It would be the last time she ever entered her own front door.

That was a Wednesday. By the time the weekend came around, Sara was incoherent more and more of the time, in part because of the brain tumors and in part because of the pain medication, which was coming in bigger doses and more frequently to manage her escalating pain.

That Sunday night, August 26, the members of Sara's Sunday school class met in Sara's backyard to sing and pray. Sara had been unable to come to church for most of that summer; this was the second or third time the church service had come to Sara. Before, she had been able to watch from her picture window. This time, she was too ill and incoherent to see the people who had come to bless her.

Sara's parents brought her friends Laura Beth and Molly to see her that evening. They had a sense that it would be the last time they would speak to their friend on this earth. In a brief, intense moment of lucidity, Sara opened her eyes and said, "I love you, and I always will. That is all."

By the next day, Monday the twenty-seventh of August, it was apparent that Sara needed more hospice care than she could get at home. An ambulance arrived that afternoon to carry her to a hospice facility.

The family hoped they had a few more days with Sara—perhaps even a few more weeks. But her earthly body only lived a few more hours. She held on just long enough to die in the wee hours of Tuesday, August 28. Is it just a coincidence that Sara's date of death—8/28—points to Romans 8:28? It doesn't seem likely. Not only was Romans 8:28 one of her favorite verses, it also seems especially appropriate to the themes of the last year of her story: "And we know that in all things God works for the good of those who love him, who have been called according to his purpose."

A year earlier, Sara had written,

I hope that if this cancer does destroy my earthly body, no one will announce it with these words:

"Sara Walker lost her battle with colon cancer on _____ "

I'm sure it's my competitive side talking, but when I hear that statement, it implies to me that cancer was the victor. Oh, no, sir! My victory is in Jesus, and I will be the victor no matter what happens to this temporary earthly body.

So for those who write church announcements, I just ask that you think about how you word that. For all Christians are conquerors, all have a final victory. I would rather read:

_____ went home to her eternal reward after battling cancer . . .

_____ received her crown of life after enduring cancer . . .

_____ has achieved the ultimate victory over cancer after battling it for years . . .

_____ has been welcomed into eternal joy after running her race with cancer with endurance . . .

True enough. Sara's father Jody once said, "You don't carry hope to the grave. Hope carries you to the grave." Sara's life infused thousands of people with hope that will carry them to the grave and far beyond.

Sara's family carried her earthly body to Unity Cemetery in Howell, Tennessee. There she was buried near her grandfather, to whom she had always been very close. And, as her funeral ended, a rainbow appeared in the sky. "Sara always loved rainbows," said Sara's mother Carol. "She always looked for them, and saw them as a sign from God. That rainbow seemed like a sign from Sara saying, 'It's all good.'"

"Sara never wanted the spotlight," her husband Brian commented, "but she was thrust into it." She prayed that her life would make a difference that was disproportionate to who she was. God answered that prayer in abundance.

"Sara's example, her willingness to step outside herself, changed the trajectory of my life and my husband's life," her friend Molly testified. "It's easy to talk to people about God when I'm telling my friend's story. She's a huge part of my testimony."

"I've never seen somebody's life and death make such a difference," was the evaluation of Sara's friend Laura Beth. And Laura Beth and Molly are just the tip of the iceberg.

In her darkest hours, Sara wondered how her suffering could possibly be worth it, how it could possibly be necessary. But Sara's life and death stand as a testimony to the enduring grace of God, who works all things—even cancer and death—to the good of those who love him. Sara surely loved him, and thanks to Sara, thousands of people love him more now than they ever did before.

Sara Walker's story is a love story. It is the story of a God who loved her and loved the world enough to answer her prayer: God, *let me make a difference for you that is utterly disproportionate to who I am.* "It is a love story from first to last," wrote Sara herself:

> It is the story of a God who loved his daughter
> beyond all human comprehension. It is the story
> of a God who loves all of us beyond our ability to
> fathom. Do you see this when you read the Bible?
> The book about a God who created a masterpiece
> in creating mankind, and who loved his people
> with such a passion that he pulled them back to
> him over and over and over and over? He pur-
> sues relentlessly because he loves us that fiercely,
> that deeply.
>
> My story is a love story. Isn't that a crazy
> thing to call it? God let my baby girl die and let

me have advanced cancer. But I know in my heart it's because he loves me so much.

See, I've always felt the love of God. I've always felt like his favorite. I've always felt it because I was blessed to be raised by the greatest set of parents ever to walk the earth.

What I've never felt is the love of people. Oh, I knew Mom and Dad loved me, and my grandparents, you know—those people who are pretty much required by law to love you—but that was about it. Just ask my mom, who the Lord knows has tried every method of extraction possible to extract my particular thorn in the flesh. I've never felt that I really mattered to anyone. Mom and Dad even told Brian about this problem of mine when he asked them for my hand in marriage. They said something to the effect of, "Sara is very special. But she doesn't think so, and she needs to be reminded quite a bit."

In the last year of Sara's life, God fulfilled that lack. By the time she left this earth, she finally understood what had been true all along: she was surrounded by people who loved her with the love of Christ. She wrote to her church body,

One of my biggest fears in having a prolonged illness is that I would be forgotten. That I would slowly but surely creep down the church prayer list, as new, very worthy, more emergent needs arose. I felt sure that it would be, "Oh, Sara

Walker . . . she's still alive . . . she hasn't asked us
for anything lately so she must be doing okay. . . .

Oh my, I ask your forgiveness. I supposed
your faithfulness in prayer for others to be like
mine. I can pray for someone for a few weeks
maybe, but then my attention is divided, my
focus wanes. Not so with you. You are teaching me the meaning of Jesus's instructions to
his disciples to "always pray, never giving up."
My church family, you are as repeatedly, stead-
fastly, boldly praying for me as much as you did
even before my official diagnosis, even in the
first few weeks of treatment. As I have failed to
make "measurable" progress in my fight against
these rogue cells, my faith has wavered. I have
become less confident in God's desire to heal
me. But you, you have told me over and over that
he is just as able to heal me completely today as
he was ten months ago. You continue to ask for
a miracle, when I feel I have gone hoarse from
asking. You *do* stand in the gap for me. You *do*
hold up my arms as they did for Moses, for my
arms are now so tired from the battle. There has
been no let-up in the private prayers, the special
collective prayer sessions, the meals, the hugs, the
cards, the endless offers to help and support in
any way possible. Tonight, as I was enveloped in
hug after hug and as people looked me deep in
the eye to ask me how I was really doing, I felt not
one minute of self-consciousness about my skin.

What a blessing! To come to a place looking very
different, very scarred, and to have my family
look right past that into my heart . . . I just have
no words.

The readers of Sara's blog took up the habit of referring to
Sara as "our Sara." It was a sign of just how much she meant
to them, and how much she belonged. It wasn't long before
she started signing many of her posts, "Your Sara"—a beautiful reminder that in the Body of Christ we all belong to
one another, just as surely as the hand belongs to the head
and the head belongs to the liver.

Thousands of people were witnesses to the life and
death of Sara Walker, and they were changed forever. Now
she is part of that great crowd of witnesses spoken of in
Hebrews: "Therefore, since we are surrounded by such a
huge *crowd of witnesses* to the life of faith, let us strip off
every weight that slows us down, especially the sin that so
easily trips us up. And let us run with *endurance* the race
God has set before us" (12:1 NLT; emphasis mine). We are
still on the journey. We are still in the race. But Sara's race is
won. She didn't lose her battle with cancer. She victoriously
joined the great cloud of witnesses.

Epilogue

by Jody Pigg

Dearest friends of our Sara,

As you can imagine, the last few years have been one continuous emotional, spiritual, heart-stretching experience. As a father who "walked through the valley of the shadow of death" with his daughter, let me speak of a single, life-changing impact.

I was, and continue to be, mesmerized by Sara's spiritual strength and stamina.

I was blessed to witness the fruition of a father's most sacred prayer and dream for his child . . . that she live life with purpose and passion, totally devoted to her Lord. Carol and I reveled in many aspects of Sara's accomplishments as a student, as an athlete, as a wife, and as a mother. But to witness her transparency of soul as she devoted her personal darkest days to encouraging others to find the joy in daily life: praying, fasting, and serving others through her writings and her "undisclosed" acts of kindness. To sit by her side and hold her close as we begged God for healing, to witness her peace and trust in God to accept his answer, it is too wondrous to describe, too sacred for words.

I have shed as many tears of thanksgiving for her steadfast faith through these fiery trials as I have the tears of heartache with her passing. I was blessed to dream *for* her in her youth, to dream *with* her as a fellow-servant of God, and now I dream *of* her, as she has taken center stage in my personal "cloud of witnesses," keeping me focused on my dream to meet her in the clouds, with her husband, her daughter, her boys, her brother, her sister, and her precious, precious mother, and all our family and friends who have placed their hope in the hands of the Mighty God, the God of the Living, the *Living God*.

Come, Lord Jesus.

And take us home.